STUART

ERRY XMAS '85

FROM MUMMY + DADDY

KU-745-273

COCKBURN'S A – Z
OF
AFTER-DINNER ENTERTAINMENT

COCKBURN'S

A – Z

OF

AFTER-DINNER
ENTERTAINMENT

Gyles Brandreth

PELHAM BOOKS

First published in Great Britain by
Pelham Books Ltd
44 Bedford Square, London WC1 3DP
1985

© Copyright Gyles Brandreth 1985

All Rights Reserved. No part of this publication may be reproduced,
stored in a retrieval system, or transmitted in any form or by any
means, electronic, mechanical, photocopying, recording or otherwise,
without the prior permission of the Copyright owner.

Brandreth, Gyles
   Cockburn's A-Z of after-dinner entertainment.
   1. Wit and humour
   I. Title
   827'.914'08   PN6151

ISBN   0 7207 1612 8

Typeset by Action Typesetting, Gloucester
Printed by Hollen Street Press, Slough and
bound by Hunter & Foulis, Edinburgh

COCKBURN'S

Cockburn's Port

As suppliers of one of the finest of all
after-dinner entertainments, Cockburn's
port, Cockburn Smithes & Co. Limited
are delighted to have sponsored this
highly entertaining encyclopaedia.

CONTENTS

CONTENTS

CONTENTS

INTRODUCTION

Cockburn's and I have been responsible for some of the most diabolical after-dinner entertainment of all time. On the night of 3 April 1982, at a dinner sponsored by them, I rose to my feet at 9.00 p.m. to try and capture the world record for the longest after-dinner speech (which I was currently sharing with Nicholas Parsons). At breakfast the following morning I sat down, a record holder by ninety minutes — and I defy anyone who endured the whole of that twelve-and-a-half hours to describe it as remotely entertaining.

True after-dinner entertainment depends first and foremost on the fostering and development of a shared experience. At its most natural, it amounts to the time-honoured formula of port and conversation. No speaker, however gifted, can hope to rival that warm and intimate ambience generated during the course of a delicious meal, elegantly presented, complimented with fine wines and good company, that culminates in the exchange of thoughts and ideas over a decanter of port, the wine that inspired much of the finest conversation ever recorded — that of Samuel Johnson.

By their very intimacy such occasions preclude more than a handful of diners and the lot falls to the after-dinner speaker to engender the bonhomie that enhances larger gatherings. Whether formal or informal, the rules that govern after-dinner speeches are the same. From preparation to presentation both require the same careful development and sensitivity if they are to succeed in capturing and amusing an audience for ten minutes or so. (You will find all these points discussed and explained in the first seven sections of this book — A–G.)

There are different styles of speech you may wish to give. There are those that say formally 'thank you' or 'goodbye' to a guest of honour; others that expound wittily on a particular theme; and there are toasts that you may be called on to propose. All have their rules and conventions that are also covered in these opening sections.

In the heart of the book you will find a range of material graded according to subject matter. This consists of anecdotes and stories, jokes and quotations that have been noted down over the years and which are included here in the hope that they might provide a departure point for your own research and collection. As well as the material itself, there are hints and tips on how it might be used and adapted to suit your purposes, to lend your speech a sparkle and zest that will leave your audience eager to hear more (the ideal point at which to conclude, by the way).

At the end of the book I have switched attention to after-dinner games, a highly popular and immensely enjoyable form of after-dinner entertainment for private dinner-parties at home.

Jonathan Swift, writing in the *Journal to Stella,* hinted at a more robust eighteenth-century environment in which post-prandial entertainment flourished: 'We were to do more business after dinner; but after dinner is after dinner

— an old saying and true, "much drinking little thinking".'

With the benefit of hindsight, nearly three centuries later, I don't think either Cockburn's or I would take great issue with that.

Gyles Brandreth.

ATTENDING TO DETAILS

Few people are born natural public speakers and regrettably fewer still seem to realize this. After-dinner speaking in particular is a skill that needs to be learnt, practised and polished before a speaker can consider himself proficient.

There are important guidelines laid down in the sections that follow but I want to start with the key to all successful after-dinner speaking — preparation.

The greatest sin for any after-dinner speaker is the sin of inadequate preparation. An after-dinner speech should be like an iceberg with eight-ninths hidden and only one-ninth showing. An after-dinner speaker is primarily an entertainer. For a few minutes (usually the fewer the better) he is on show to amuse, engage and just occasionally enlighten his audience. He does this by a delicate combination of subject matter and delivery, ingredients blended and measured with the same careful precision as those used by the chef in the kitchen to create the dinner that has just been served. The enjoyment of the dinner comes from savouring the finished dishes and the same should be true of the speeches that follow. The hard work in both cases must be over before either is offered to the assembled company.

It doesn't matter whether you've been invited to speak to a gathering of international nuclear physicists or the Nether Wallop branch of the Tiddlywinks Association, your preparation will need to be meticulous in both cases if your speech is going to succeed. Without careful, attentive planning and structuring your speech will lack that essential balance and shape that marks it out as appealing to one specific audience.

Here are some practical hints of getting to grips with a speech which have served me well over the years and which I hope may be of some use to you as well.

Know Your Audience

1. Always remember that you have been invited to please your audience, not yourself. You can satisfy your own ego at home, but as a speaker it is your duty to stimulate and entertain those who have been kind enough to ask you to speak.

2. Adapt your material to suit that audience. A speech given at an annual rugby club dinner would obviously be quite inappropriate delivered to a Townswomen's Guild. Similarly one that had an old boys' reunion in stitches would have little appeal when given to a large commercial convention when few of those present know each other. The age of your audience is a crucial factor too. An audience that appreciates references to Pat Boone may be less enamoured by an analysis of the career of Boy George.

3. Try and assess the mood of your audience. Are they going to be jubilant after a year of record profits? Or will they be smarting from their club's third successive year of relegation? This is a matter of tact. Different occasions

5

require different kinds of speeches. Treat your audience as you would a friend and make their feelings of paramount importance.

4. Remember that your task is to please as many of your audience as possible, not just a small clique you may be trying to impress. No speaker can count himself a success if he has one table in hoots of laughter at the expense of

everyone else. You may not succeed in pleasing all the audience all of the time, but you can certainly try.

5. You should always fulfil the purpose of your speech. Whether it's to offer a vote of thanks, say goodbye to a friend, congratulate a company on its sales record, or propose a toast, you must never become so engrossed with your own oratory that you forget the reason you're speaking in the first place. The same rule applies when it comes to compiling the speech — stick to your subject.

In my experience the most satisfactory way to prepare a speech is to let your ideas build up over a period of days or even weeks. Leave it to the last minute and it's likely to sound rushed and disjointed.

A convenient way of starting to organize your thoughts is to write your subject in capital letters in the centre of a large sheet of paper and then (literally) write around your central theme. You can jot down quotations, newspaper stories, personal anecdotes, anything that comes to mind.

Once you've explored the topic in this random way you can begin arranging the material into a more cogent structure by dividing the speech into three categories: Introduction, Discussion of the Main Subject, and Conclusion. Now allocate material to each category, ruthlessly eliminating anything that on reflection departs from your subject no matter how amusing it may be. Your final selection should aim to be entertaining, stimulating, but above all, relevant to your theme.

The same ruthlessness must apply with the length of your speech. An after-dinner speech should last between five and fifteen minutes, though it is always better to err on the side of brevity. No one will ever complain that your speech is too short and as Lord Reading once advised,

'Always be shorter than anyone dared hope.'

By their nature after-dinner speeches include a generous portion of humour which leads to the natural temptation to mould a speech around a few favourite jokes rather than tailoring any jokes to suit the speech. This discipline is vital all the same. Ideally all the jokes or stories you decide to include should be both original and relevant. A joke that interrupts the flow of a speech should be left out; if it can't be incorporated into the natural cadence it doesn't belong, no matter how funny you think it is.

If you decide to tell a joke or story you heard related by a well-known comedian (and the best jokes and anecdotes are usually those the audience *haven't* heard before) always acknowledge your source. Like as not someone in the audience will recognize it and will dub you a plagiarist if you pretend it's your own. What's more, if the audience are told that the joke is one of Cannon and Ball's, for example, they're more likely to sit up and listen.

Wherever possible, though, you should try to make your material sound fresh and original. If you include at least one new item of your own, you'll have injected something of your own personality into the speech which the audience will be able to take home as a particular memory of what you said to them.

It may be that you feel a moment of seriousness is needed if you have an important point to get across (though with after-dinner speaking moments like these should be the exception rather than the rule). This can be heightened by a careful juxtaposition with a moment of great hilarity. It needn't, indeed it shouldn't, be pompous or solemn. Provided you are sincere in what you say, and having said it move quickly on to lighter material the audience will register your change of tone and your point will have the impact it merits.

Your Sources
Much of your preparation will be filled by compiling material from a wide variety of sources. It doesn't matter that much of this will have to be rejected when you come to finalize the structure. It's far better to have too much from which to choose than too little. (Though you should remember the warning not to overrun your set time by trying to pack too much into your speech. Audience laughter and other interruptions need to be accounted for as well if you are going to stick rigidly to your schedule.) Among the most widely used sources you will probably want to include the following:

1. *Television and Radio:* Television and radio programmes can often trigger ideas as well as providing useful source material. Try to build on what you hear, using it as a point of departure for your observations. You might introduce a light-hearted comparison between British and North American English by saying, 'I was listening to a talk on the difficulties of learning English on the radio the other day and it struck me that . . .' If any of the audience happened to hear the same programme you will have established a common point of reference and to those who didn't hear it you'll give the impression of having a mind eager to follow up someone else's thoughts with ideas of your own.

2. *Magazines:* These provide a useful source of opinion and information on a broad range of subjects. Use them freely as reference material, but if you decide to quote from one directly, you must always acknowledge your

9

source. This general rule applies to all source material. An acknowledgment in no way detracts from your speech, whereas failing to give one can soon land you in hot water if someone in the audience recognizes the source and announces the fact to the rest of the company. Keep cuttings of amusing and interesting articles for future use.

3. *Newspapers:* Newspapers have the great advantage of being up-to-date. Your speech will have a sense of immediacy if you include a reference to something or someone currently in the news. Events less than twenty-four hours old are probably too recent since some of your audience may not have heard about them, won't understand your reference and will start whispering to their neighbours for enlightenment. The local press can be an invaluable source of background information if you are speaking away from home and a couple of hours spent reading a local paper will give you a feel for points of local interest to which your audience will warm when you show even a modest awareness of their current affairs.

4. *Dictionaries of Quotations:* If you have a specific quotation in mind always double-check it in a dictionary of quotations which you'll find in your nearest library, if you haven't one at home. It doesn't take a great deal of effort to make sure that you have the correct wording and have attributed the comment to the right person. Slips in either case are signs of poor preparation and there may be someone listening who's more than eager to correct your mistake. It's also important when quoting people directly to make sure that you aren't taking their remark out of context or giving it the wrong connotations. Again a dictionary of quotations should help verify these points.

   This is also a convenient point to mention the

importance that needs to be attached to the correct pronunciation of words both in foreign languages and in
English. Certain English names have a pronunciation
peculiar to themselves and pity the speaker who in-
advertently gets this wrong. Take the name Cockburn for
instance. Any speaker who accents the '-ck', making the
famous port sound like a chicken left to char in the oven,
will rapidly lose his audience's confidence with such an
elementary mistake. On the other hand there is no reason
why a special feature cannot be made of unusual pro-
nunciations. Anyone talking about the idiosyncracies of
English might open with a lighthearted example of the
difficulties presented by pronunciation. Perhaps a short
anecdote, or a limerick, would serve as a succinct
example, in the case of the name Cockburn's it might be:

For years a gourmet near Wockburn,
Stocked his cellar from a merchant in Hockburn,
Who was free to select
Any Champagne or Sekt,
But for port was asked always for Cockburn's.

From this the speaker could move into the broader
discussion of why 'plough' and 'cough', though spelt with
similar endings should be pronounced differently.

5. *Reference Books:* Public libraries stock encyclopaedias
and a wide selection of key reference books on most
subjects. Use these to check any factual information you
want to include in your speech and make a note of the
sources to back up what you are going to say.

6. *Experts:* In the event of a reference book failing to
support a fact you wish to include there is no reason why
you shouldn't approach an acknowledged expert in the

field. As long as you enclose a stamped, addressed envelope and make your question as clear and simple as possible most experts are usually perfectly happy to confirm or correct your information. Never ask for confidential information and never place the expert in a position where he or she may become drawn into a controversy of your making (though here again this type of debate is hardly the stuff of which successful after-dinner speeches are made).

7. *Personal Experiences:* For an after-dinner speaker these will probably be the most appropriate source material. Remarks you overhear, incidents that amuse you, things that have happened to you, your family or friends can be noted down and used to bring a personal flavour to your speech, one that's fresh and original and free from questions of authenticity or credibility.

You'll need to use your judgement in how you use or adapt any source material bearing in mind the nature of your audience. Anything that any reasonable person might take as being even vaguely offensive should be deleted. You may raise one or two laughs with a smutty joke or gentle dig at a religious or minority group, but these will be a hollow return for the ill feeling you're likely to generate in most of the audience — which brings me back to one of my earlier points, that the after-dinner speaker is there to entertain first and foremost. Offending an audience is hardly the most courteous way of repaying their hospitality.

As I hope you'll appreciate preparing a speech is not a task to be taken lightly. You will need time and you must work at it. When an eminent American senator was asked how long he had been working on a particularly successful political speech, he replied: 'Twenty years.'

After-dinner speaking may have a different objective but there is no room for complacency. You'd better get started right away!

BEGINNINGS AND OPENINGS

Sam Goldwyn, discussing a forthcoming film with his team, once told them, 'What we want is a story that begins with an earthquake and works its way up to a climax.' Mr Goldwyn may not have been a man noted for using a full stop where an exclamation mark would do but his sentiment could usefully be applied to after-dinner speaking. Begin forcefully and end triumphantly.

Ways of closing speeches are covered in the section that follows but it's worth mentioning here that your opening and closing remarks are equally important. The way you choose to begin engages your audience's attention for the main body of your speech and the way you end colours the impression you leave them with. Good openings and closings are essential and many speakers work on them at the same time, so that they link convincingly and effectively. Of course it's equally important that they also relate to the kernel of what you are saying; the best openings and closing in the history of after-dinner speaking are wasted and, worse still, irrelevant if they have nothing to do with your main theme. So much for the two together — for now let's concentrate on how to begin.

Think for a moment of the setting in which your after-dinner speech is going to be given. You will all have enjoyed (at least you hope you'll have enjoyed) a fairly substantial meal. Most guests will have been sitting for an hour or more. Some may take this opportunity to move back their chairs and stretch their legs. The port will be circulating (Cockburn's if you're lucky). Cigars will be searched for, will be offered and lit. And into this atmosphere you get to your feet to speak wittily and amusingly for ten minutes or so.

Your beginning has to arouse your audience's attention at the outset but you must take into consideration the need for those still sitting to make themselves comfortable, in order to appreciate what you are saying to the full. Speak up, speak clearly and engage their interest by your opening comments and they will be with you for the rest of the speech. It's far easier to win their attention at the outset than struggle to capture it halfway through.

Before suggesting some of the ways in which you might choose to begin, here are a few of the pitfalls to avoid.

1. Tired old clichés along the lines of 'Unaccustomed as I am to public speaking . . .' or 'A funny thing happened to me on the way here this evening' will strangle a speech at birth.

2. Never tell an audience that you're going to be brief. It's very unlikely that they'll believe you and it's every bit as unlikely that you will be brief. Everyone will be disappointed, and the speech, no matter how good it might have been, will be a catastrophe.

3. Any attempt at false modesty by asserting that you have no idea why you were invited to speak only begs the question who might have been asked instead. There may also be someone in the room eager to answer that everyone else was booked, or worse still they might share in your bewilderment at the choice of speaker.

4. Open confidentially. Don't rush or gabble, but speak forcefully and with purpose. You can modify your tone to suit the atmosphere once everyone is settled but don't be tentative when you begin speaking. As Oliver Wendell warned: 'Don't strew your pathway with those dreadful errs.'

The way you begin a speech will vary according to the subject, the audience you are addressing and your relationship with them. Although general guidelines can be given, it's always far more effective if you can devise an original slant of your own. That said, here are some alternative opening gambits which might inspire you:

A Starter for Ten: Questions immediately engage your audience's attention by involving them, or appearing to involve them, directly in your train of thought. They can provide a neat and amusing way of launching into your speech. A speaker addressing a Young Farmers' dinner with some wry comments on the EEC agricultural policy might open with a question like: 'Have you ever stopped to think how much a country's cheeses tell us about its people?' A question like this provides a convenient link with the dinner that's just been served (assuming that cheese is offered on the menu). It also shows some common interest with the audience, some of whom may well be dairy producers. And it leads into a more discursive discussion of our EEC partners in a way that the audience are most likely to appreciate, perhaps by way of one of General de Gaulle's most celebrated comments: 'The French will only be united under the threat of danger. Nobody can simply bring together a country that has 265 kinds of cheese.'

Short and Sharp: A single, powerful opening sentence can be a particularly effective way of moving into your main theme. You might be giving a talk on National Service when a statement like: 'If it moved you saluted it, if it didn't move you painted it white — that's what the army taught me,' should immediately set the scene for your audience and probably ring a few bells of recognition as well.

Begin with a Laugh: When they work, humorous openings are an ideal way of putting your audience at ease. When they fail everyone can be on edge waiting for the next calamity. So be careful.

For a joke to work at the opening of a speech the audience must be able to hear it and must understand that it's meant to be funny. Remember that some of them will still be getting comfortable as you start to speak, so your timing and delivery will need all your concentration if the joke is going to come off. Jokes that aren't strictly relevant are best avoided altogether. The last thing you want is people whispering: 'Why did he start talking about horse racing when he's on to cricket now?' after you've just delivered a devastatingly witty pun on the Royal Box at Ascot.

Poems and Quotations: With a little judicious research you should be able to find a suitable quotation to open virtually any speech. Again it's vital that the quotation is strictly relevant to what you're going on to say and allows you to move swiftly and smoothly into the main part of the speech.

For instance a lighthearted look at the difficulties that can arise from not knowing the details of particular customs or codes of etiquette might open with this charming example in verse, which has the added merit of dovetailing perfectly with the port that will be circulating at the time.

> It was Christmas Day at the College
>   and the port was freeing the wit,
> when someone (what absence of knowledge!)
>   said Cockburn the way it is writ.
>
> Those clever old dons then made sport,
>   They chortled in donnish derision
> at their colleague who'd never been taught
>   the su'tler points of elision.
>
> But the Dean with compassion was wrought.
>   He said, gently, 'Young man, you should know
> when seeking perfection in port,
>   one doesn't say cock, one says co.

(If you use a direct quotation from any source, remember to give full credit to the author, however obscure the quotation may appear.)

Brief extracts from poems can be a concise way of introducing your subject. Anyone speaking on the subject of wit would be hard put to better Pope's famous couplet from his *Essay on Criticism:*

> True wit is nature to advantage dress'd,
> What oft was thought, but ne'er so well express'd

In introducing the main theme after this the speaker might comment: 'That couplet was written in 1711 by Alexander Pope, who in my opinion was himself one of this country's greatest exponents of wit.' He is then free to move in whichever direction he has chosen, confident that the audience know exactly what he is talking about.

The Personal Touch: If you are a member of the group to whom you are speaking or have close ties with them, don't be afraid to acknowledge this when you open. Similarly if you sincerely feel that a significant compliment has been paid in asking you to speak, say so and give your reasons. You audience will appreciate your remarks and you'll have established a common bond with them by showing due respect for the body to which they belong.

The Stunt: You need to be careful with this one too. If you're unlucky enough to be the last in a succession of speakers the stunt might just help wake up the audience

and grab their attention while you deliver a few brief words to wind up the dinner. However, stunts that back-fire can leave everyone feeling terribly embarrassed and need considerable skill afterwards to retrieve the situation. There are speakers who open by referring to a sheet of notes which they suddenly tear up and disperse like confetti around them. In the right setting and with the right audience it can be hilarious; in the wrong circum-stances it will be a nightmare. It's all a matter of judge-ment and unless no other course is open to you, stunts are best left to others. That's why they come at the end of this list.

Now for ways of coming to the end of your speech.

CLOSING REMARKS

If your audience remember anything of what you have said it is most likely to be the end of your speech, which is why your closing remarks are so important. Whether you choose an ending that is humorous, thought-provoking, or surprising it must effectively conclude what you have been talking about and needs to carry the same impetus as your opening. No speech, no matter how effective the opening or the treatment of the main theme, can be counted a success if it ends with a damp squib.

A weak conclusion either shows that you've run out of ideas or that you have shown so little interest in the audience you are addressing that your only aim is to get the speech over and done with. Any speaker who ends with a 'That's all folks' attitude deserves the disappointment with which he's bound to be met. You owe it to your hosts to wind up your speech as elegantly and engagingly as you can. If you begin with a flourish, you must end with a flourish too. You certainly won't want it said of your speech: 'It had a happy ending — everyone was so glad when it was over.'

In many respects the principles governing closing remarks mirror those mentioned under ways to begin, as you'll see from the ones given below.

Funny Ending: In some ways trying to end a speech with a joke is even riskier than trying to open with one. If it falls flat you've nothing to follow that might redeem you and you'll leave the audience with the painful spectacle of you taking your seat to spasmodic applause because no one is sure whether or not they're meant to laugh and whether you have finished speaking.

Jokes that lead on directly from the main body of your speech stand a greater chance of succeeding because they will have a direct relevance to your theme. As a general rule 'gentle' humour is preferable to aiming for an all-or-nothing burst of raucous laughter. Probably the safest way of using a funny ending is to keep it light and deliver it positively and clearly. Leaving your audience with a smile is just as rewarding as sitting down to a chorus of belly-laughs.

A Closing Story: If you can find an anecdote that illustrates the main theme of your speech, by all means use it to round off the evening. Providing it genuinely encapsulates the main thrust of your message it can be a particularly effective way of closing.

If you are speaking at a dinner held in honour of someone, or are paying a personal tribute to a friend or colleague, an affectionate anecdote that brings out the best of their qualities will meet with everyone's approval and will round off your remarks gracefully.

A Final Quote: A relevant quotation can work as effectively at the close of a speech as at the opening (providing it really is relevant). You shouldn't use one for the beginning *and* one for the end, that too can suggest a lack of imagination. Again you must always acknowledge your source.

Food for Thought: After-dinner speaking lends itself less happily to thought-provoking subjects that in other areas might effectively stir the consciences and rally the emotions of the audience. However, if in entertaining your audience you hit on an amusing formula that leaves them with a question to ponder by all means use it. A speaker at a cricket club dinner might conclude some thoughts on the state of the international game by commenting that the oldest international cricket match in the world is played between Canada and the USA. That should set some of the audience thinking.

Surprise, Surprise: A word of caution here too — gimmicks and stunts should really be used as a final resort and then they're best left to speakers with a fair amount of after-dinner experience behind them. If your speech has gone well you won't want to spoil it by a stunt that misfires. If it hasn't gone well you'd do better to come to your planned conclusion and sit down smartly. If you apply your mind and start planning well in advance you're almost certain to hit on a more suitable and more acceptable way of coming to a conclusion.

In the final analysis you should aim to close your speech with something that is brief, relevant and, if possible, original — always remembering that you want your audience to remember *what* you say, not the *methods* you use to say it. Follow Claudius's advice to Polonius in *Hamlet,* 'More matter with less art', and you shouldn't go far wrong.

DRINK TO ME ONLY

As an after-dinner speaker one of the commonest duties you'll be called on to perform is the proposing of toasts and that's why I'd like to touch on toasts and toasting here.

Toasts fall into two broad categories — loyal and patriotic toasts, and social toasts. Each has it conventions which should be observed.

Loyal and Patriotic Toasts

These require no embellishments. They are formal toasts to the Queen and occasionally other members of the royal family. The chairman or the toastmaster proposes the loyal toast and should simply say: 'The Queen', or if he insists on saying more, the most he should say is: 'The Queen, God bless her.'

If a second loyal toast follows it should be to other members of the royal family and should be as brief as the first, and once again no speech is required.

Patriotic toasts are usually given at dinners connected with the Armed Forces. Here the toast can be given collectively: 'Her Majesty's Forces', or it can be offered to just one of the services, either 'The Royal Navy', 'The Army', or 'The Royal Air Force'. Normally no speech is required with patriotic toasts, but in the event of the chairman proposing the toast to Her Majesty's Forces which is then replied to by one member of each service, a very short speech will be required *before* the toast.

The motto that has always impressed me with patriotic speeches is: 'Be brief, be sincere, be seated.'

Social Toasts
Though adding an element of formality to social occasions, social toasts are less rigidly structured than loyal or patriotic toasts and allow the proposer some scope in saying a few words before proposing the toast.

For an after-dinner speaker social toasts are most likely to be given in honour of individuals or institutions and he can afford to dwell for a moment on the subject of the toast in a light-hearted and good-humoured way.

If a colleague is retiring after forty years with the company, his farewell dinner is an obvious occasion to acknowledge his long service and important contribution to the firm. Intricate details of the way he revised the internal auditing in 1958, important as they may be, would lend too ponderous a tone to what is meant to be an entertaining occasion. However, an affectionate leg-pull about the way the office junior had to show him how to work the new word processor, coupled with a brief reference to his pioneering work in earlier years will acknowledge his endeavours without sounding like a curriculum vitae. Your speech needs really to perform two roles: to thank the person you are toasting and wish him a happy retirement, and to lead directly and smoothly into the toast itself.

You should aim to keep your comments prior to the toast fairly brief; in my view two minutes is the maximum for a speech of this sort. As Lord Butler once remarked, a toast should be like a woman's dress — long enough to cover everything but short enough to be interesting. And when it comes to the toast itself you need only say: 'To Jack', or in the case of a couple celebrating their silver wedding anniversary, for instance, 'I'd now like you all to join me in raising our glasses and wishing them the same health and happiness in the future. Here's to David and Mary.'

This last point leads me on to one of the vital details of all toasts. Make sure that everyone has their glass full *before* you begin to speak. Nothing is worse than a toast interrupted by people frantically trying to top up their glasses and whispering down the table for something to put in them.

Proposing toasts is an important and pleasant task, but it is not without its dangers. The story goes that on one occasion a senior British diplomat who was attending a trade delegation dinner in the Soviet Union decided to propose an after-dinner toast to his hosts in Russian. Though he had spent some time with a phrase book preparing the short speech, his mind went blank when the time came to get to his feet. He could not recall the Russian for 'Ladies and Gentlemen'. Suddenly he noticed the toilets at the back of the room. Here were the very words he sought printed in large white letters on each door.

Unfortunately the toast did not seem to go down too well with his hosts, so he asked a colleague who had been in Russia some time to explain his chilly reception. His friend laughed, and replied: 'Because you began your speech by addressing them as "Male and Female Conveniences".'

The diplomat's unfortunate loss of memory at a crucial moments should not obscure the fact that he had at least

prepared something in advance.

Extempore toasts, on the other hand, can run a greater risk of going wrong. At another diplomatic dinner, prepared toasts were proposed by various diners to both the ladies of the East and those of the West. At this point, a young diplomat unwisely decided to contribute a toast of his own, and with great seriousness entreated the other diners to 'drink a toast to the two hemispheres of ladies.' His career was not advanced by that unfortunate infelicity.

However, for a masterpiece of diplomacy and a shining example of an impromptu toast that can only be called a triumph here is an anecdote told of that great American statesman, Benjamin Franklin.

During his time as the American emissary in France, he

was dining one evening at Versailles with the English Ambassador and the French Minister. The meal ended and the formal toasts began:

'George III,' began the English Ambassador, 'who, like the sun at its meridian, shines brightly forth and enlightens the whole world.'

'His Royal Highness Louis XVI,' continued the French Minister, 'who, like the moon, pours forth his rays and influences the entire globe.'

Then came Franklin's turn to propose a toast.

'George Washington,' he said, 'commander of the American armies, who, like Joshua of old, commanded the sun and the moon to stand still, and they obeyed him.'

On the whole I feel that the toasts that work best are those that come from the heart rather than from a collection of tired old chestnuts. However, if you are really stuck for the right words and think that any of the toasts that I've noted down here say exactly what you want to say, I'm happy that they'll be of use. The mood you choose to strike is entirely your own affair, all I will say is that whichever toast you select it must tie in with the sentiment and sense of your preamble.

General Toasts — These are really toasts to everyone present. Most are light-hearted though many contain more than a grain of truth:

> Let us drink to the kind of troubles which last only as long as our New Year's resolutions.

> Here's to middle age, when we start to do things because they are good for us, rather than because we like doing them.

> Let us drink to excellence; the ability not to do

28

extraordinary things, but to do ordinary things extra-ordinarily well.

May Lady Fortune smile on you all for the rest of your lives; but never her daughter — Miss Fortune.

May every man become what he thinks himself to be.

May the Lord love us but not call us too soon.

Drink! and pray that all our meals may be fun as well as fuel.

Toasts to Friends and Acquaintances — These are best covered by the simple formula of naming the friend or friends at the end of your brief introductory speech. However, here are a few alternatives that may be fitting:

Let us drink to the health of an old friend. May she live for a thousand years, and may we all be there to count them.

May your joys be as deep as the great ocean, and your sorrows as light as its spray.

To absent friends, God bless them all.

(A toast to a principal guest might be presented in this way:

To our honoured guest, for a friend of our friend is doubly our friend.)

Toasts to Wives and Families — These are affectionate toasts offered with a twinkle in the eye and a heart full of cheer:

Here's to our sweethearts and our wives,
May our sweethearts soon become our wives,
And our wives still remain our sweethearts.

To woman: the only beloved autocrat who governs
without law; and decides without appeal.

Here's to children. Not only are they a great comfort
in our old age, but they help us to reach it faster too.

I hope these may inspire you to create toasts of your own.
Personal tributes will always ring true and often truer than
those culled from other people. Remember Polonius and
say what you mean succinctly and sincerely.

ELEMENTARY PRECAUTIONS

Preparing your speech is one matter, delivering it is another, but between the two comes an equally important stage — taking steps to make sure that you and your speech are received as favourably as possible. That's what I want to touch on here.

If you're speaking in familiar surroundings to an audience you know and who know you, many of these precautionary words will be unnecessary. For inexperienced speakers about to give an after-dinner speech away from home, I hope that these tips will help remove some of the difficulties that the unwary have encountered in the past. All of these are matters of common sense and on paper look almost too obvious to be worth mentioning. In the excitement of the moment, however, as the butterflies are starting to flex their wings in your tummy, it's easy to overlook a simple precaution and risk spoiling your speech.

How You Look

This may hardly seem to be a precaution, but you should always try to look at your best when invited to be an after-dinner speaker. As Mae West might have said, 'There's a difference between good looks and looking good.' While after-dinner speakers don't necessarily need the former, they should aspire to the latter — for two important reasons. The first is simply a matter of courtesy. Your appearance should compliment that of your hosts. If the other men are wearing black tie, you should be similarly dressed. If everyone else is going to be wearing lounge suits, a dinner jacket is obviously going to be out of place and you should wear a lounge suit too. Your clothes should be smart without being ostentatious as well. The second reason is that initial impressions count for a great deal when your audience see you for the first time and if you dress in a manner that conforms to the occasion, they will feel more at ease immediately; dress in a slovenly or careless way and they have a right to fear the worst.

Using Notes

It's inadvisable to try and read an after-dinner speech from a written copy. Politicians may get away with this when giving political speeches, but they generally have the experience and skill to make a speech sound reasonably alive and interesting, even if they are reading it word for word; furthermore they are usually speaking with a very different purpose in mind. After-dinner speakers on the other hand need a lightness of touch, a hint of spontaneity and a degree of flexibility to deliver their speeches in an appealing way. Reading a speech will almost certainly make it sound wooden and monotonous.

By the time you come to deliver it, the structure of your speech ought to be clear in your mind. You may feel confident to give it without any notes at all, but a sheet of paper bearing the main headings can be reassuring and will prevent you rambling away from your subject. If you intend using quotations, these can also be written out in full, so that you get the wording absolutely right.

Some speakers like to write their notes on cards though this does carry the joint risks of getting the cards in the wrong order if you drop them and of putting down two cards by accident, and so losing your way. By writing your notes on a single sheet of paper, these problems are eliminated.

Don't attempt to hide the fact that you are using notes, simply hold them comfortably at waist height and lift them up when you want to refer to them. If you're reading a quotation the audience will see that you're not relying on your memory, and that too should impress them with your thoroughness and attention to detail.

Pre-speech Checks

Once the evening arrives and you find yourself at your venue there are a number of checks you can carry out to forestall very basic mishaps, which are listed here:

1. See that you have your notes if you're using them and reading glasses if you need them.

2. Make sure you have a handkerchief and a glass of water. Apart from allowing you to wipe your nose and take a sip of water, these can be useful props if you want to introduce a natural pause in your delivery to let a remark sink home and give your audience time to respond.

3. See if there is a clock you can easily keep an eye on. If there isn't, place your watch on the table where you can see it. Don't keep looking at it, but glance at it once or twice as you speak to confirm that you aren't in danger of running over your time limit. If you've planned your speech properly, allowing optimistically for audience response, you should have a good idea how long it lasts; even so your watch or a clock is a useful double-check.

33

4. If you're going to be using a microphone make sure that it works and find out how to use it before the proceedings get under way. Check too that it's switched on before you get up to speak, though be careful that it isn't turned on so far in advance that it broadcasts the conversation that is going on round you at the end of the last course.

5. Try to get a feel for the room where you'll be speaking. Test the acoustics. If the room is large and you will be addressing a sizeable audience your style may need to be more declamatory than normal. If it's small, you will need a more intimate delivery.

34

Notice too how the audience are seated, so that you can make eye contact with those at the sides and the back as well as those seated in front of you. And once you begin speaking, don't ask if the people at the back can hear you, look at them; if they seem to be straining to catch what you're saying, speak up.

6. One final but essential tip, even if you're only going to be speaking for a few minutes, is to make yourself comfortable and visit the lavatory before you start your speech. It was Edward VIII who commented that one of the most important lessons he learned from his early years in public life was never to miss the chance to spend a penny, and after working to prepare your speech, you owe it to yourself to see that you deliver it without the explosive desire to dash to the loo.

F LUENCY AND FRESHNESS

The delivery of an after-dinner speech is not something to be left to chance. In order to work to the best effect, your speech needs to sound fluent and fresh if your audience are going to enjoy it to the full. You can take steps to improve the clarity of your diction and to give your delivery variety, but success comes primarily from presenting yourself as an interested and interesting person, and this is achieved by a combination of the way you use both your voice and your whole body to communicate your emotions and ideas.

How You Sound
Pause for a moment and consider the extent to which *you* judge other people by their voices. Are they interesting to listen to, or is their delivery flat and monotonous? The same judgement will be made of you after you have spoken your first couple of sentences, which is why it's important to let your voice express what you want to say pleasantly and engagingly.

Here are some hints that may help you use your voice to its full advantage:

1. Never be concerned about your accent. It's not only

your birthright, it goes a long way towards reflecting your personality. Don't try and disguise an accent since whatever voice you manage to create is almost certain to sound artificial and if it wavers the audience will see right through you anyway. It is the clarity of the way you speak, not your accent which is important.

2. Resist the temptation to rush your words to get the speech finished as soon as possible. As a rule, you should aim to speak slightly slower than you would in a normal conversation. This doesn't mean that your speech should be punctuated by frequent and meaningless pauses. Stopping half-way through each sentence, because you think it sounds professional is a mistake; it doesn't sound professional at all and it soon becomes very tedious to the listener. You should aim to let your delivery flow naturally, while keeping it calm, clear and precise. An average rate of 110 words a minute is about the right speed for most people, but the surest way to check for yourself is to record part of your speech and experiment with varying speeds until you find the tempo that suits you best.

3. Try not to let your voice remain at the same pitch throughout your speech. A continuous deep, booming voice can be just as irritating as a high-pitched one. Bring life and variety into the way you speak and you'll bring life into your audience as well.

4. One common mistake is to let your voice drop at the end of a sentence. If you know this is a fault you share, try to correct it with practice.

5. Learn to emphasise the important words and phrases, either by pausing before them, or by raising your voice slightly. Selective emphasis will help to communicate the

main themes of what you are saying.

6. Guard against shouting at your audience. If you think that some of them may have difficulty hearing you, raise your voice slightly, but it's more effective to speak clearly and distinctly than to raise your volume and lose control of your voice altogether.

Voice exercises can help develop your articulation and two simple ones are given below:

1. Your tongue, teeth, lips and jaw all have their part to play in the clarity of your diction. Try repeating this phrase with a friend: 'A nice cream bun.'
If you actually say: 'An ice-cream bun', you know you've got some practice in store.

2. Notice in this exercise how a change of emphasis can alter the whole meaning of what you are saying. Look at the different interpretations given to the sentence: 'You know I like carrots', all of which come from laying stress on a different word.
'*You* know I like carrots' (*You* know, but others might not).
'You *know* I like carrots' (You *know* — there's no avoiding the fact).
'You know *I* like carrots' (*I* like them, though others might not).
'You know I *like* carrots' (I like them, yes, but do I have to have them all the time?)
'You know I like *carrots*' (but did you know I like courgettes too?)

3. Experiment with the strength and volume of your voice too. Pick a sentence from your speech and begin by whispering it so that only someone sitting at your table could possibly hear what you are saying. Gradually increase the volume as you repeat it, so that your voice is loud enough to fill a small room, then a large hall and finally loud enough to carry in an open-air meeting.

Listening to newsreaders on radio and television can teach you a lot about ways of modulating your voice to make each new idea sound bright and interesting. When you consider the number of items covered in a news bulletin, newsreaders manage to lend new emphasis to each, so that their delivery never becomes monotonous, or more seriously, confusing. Freshness of intonation and clarity of voice are two distinct qualities which go to make the best newsreaders and the same hold true in the make-up of the best after-dinner speakers.

How Your Body Responds

As an after-dinner speaker you are also a communicator and the way your body communicates the emotion of your speech is every bit as important as the way your voice does. There's also the other fact that if you don't pay attention to the way you stand or the expression on your face these could be a positive hindrance by distracting the audience from what you are saying. Obviously you don't want to be fidgeting about like a badly controlled puppet; all you should aim to do is to appear relaxed and to respond naturally.

At the start of your speech, why not smile at the audience? You never know, they might smile back and what better way to open your acquaintance with them? Similarly if they are grinning at what you're saying, allow yourself to smile at the humour too. Your amusement, indeed all your emotions, will be very infectious and a skilled speaker will learn to use his face and eyes in particular to convey the sentiment behind his words.

Eye contact is very important, it forms a bond between you and those listening, and by establishing eye contact throughout your audience you'll be bringing everyone into your confidence and involving the whole gathering.

Don't be afraid to use your hands to make a point as well. A clear gesture can be a useful accompaniment to an important point. Watch that you don't get into the habit of using gestures instead of words; you're there to speak not give a mime. But gestures performed just before a point you want to emphasize can heighten that point with great effect.

Even your head can be moved to make a suitable gesture, looking over your shoulder, closing your eyes — the scope is far wider than a nod for 'yes' and a shake for 'no'. As with all these gestures be careful not to let them become annoying mannerisms, and if you can bear to face it, ask a friend to tell you frankly if you have any mannerisms already that need to be curbed. You may not enjoy this, but it's always better to find out sooner rather than later.

You can get a good idea of which gestures work effectively and which don't from watching other speakers live or on television. If you do try to emulate any of these, see if you can make them your own by adapting them to suit your personality. They're likely to be much more effective for your purposes used that way.

Ground Rules

As you'll have gathered there are certain fundamental rules of after-dinner speaking which help to keep speakers on the right track. So before moving to the final section of tips and hints (the one that deals with the unexpected) here is a checklist of 'do's and 'don'ts' that covers what has been said already and adds amplification to a number of points.

Do's

1. Do try to appear as human as possible. Don't be afraid to show a few nerves. There aren't many people (professional speakers included) who can stand up in front of an audience without being a little nervous. The trick is to use this to positive effect. If you seem arrogant to your audience, you will only alienate them. Admit the importance of the occasion, show a little vulnerability, and they will warm to you.

2. Do know your subject as fully as possible and take the trouble to verify any facts or quotations you intend using. Bluff is no replacement for genuine research and if you're found to be bluffing you will have a lot of explaining to do.

3. Do allow for an element of flexibility in your speech. Respond to the unexpected. In that way you stand a chance of staying in control of the situation rather than being thrown completely.

4. Do be sincere. It's pointless feigning enthusiasm for something when your heart patently isn't in it. If you speak about something you believe in your sincerity will always show through.

5. Do be direct. The last thing an audience wants to listen

43

to is a random, meandering talk without any purpose or direction. Say what you have to say succinctly and precisely, not by putting the minimum amount of thought into the maximum amount of words.

6. Do speak loudly and clearly, so that everyone can catch what you're saying. Even if your speech is the best since Pericles's funeral oration, it will still be to no avail if half the audience can't hear you.

7. Do try to inject at least one fresh and original element into your speech. The personal touch is terribly important and in terms of winning over an audience is worth more than the best of the material culled from others.

8. Do try to make your speech topical as well. If you are speaking to a local society, use the local papers to find out something about them and where they live. Talk to your neighbours at dinner too, and see what you can learn from them. This all helps to give your speech colour and vitality.

Don'ts

1. Don't reveal the contents of your speech to anyone before you give it. It's important to retain the element of surprise, and the whole impact of what you're about to say could be ruined by someone to whom you confided the information, or the joke, laughing prematurely or nudging his neighbours.

2. Don't drop names. This will only make you appear haughty and will do little to draw your audience closer to you.

3. Don't always make yourself the subject of the stories you tell. If they happened to someone else, give that person the credit.

4. Don't try to tell stories using accents or dialects unless you are a really accomplished impersonator (in which case you probably won't be needing the advice in this book anyway). Getting the accent wrong or mixed up will only detract from your story.

5. Don't use an obscure word where a plain one will do. Your speech should be easy to understand without being obviously patronising to your audience. It's simply that 'Perceive ocularly in advance of an abrupt saltation' doesn't have quite the same ring to it as 'Look before you leap'.

6. Don't include any material in your speech that might be construed as being in bad taste. There are some people who take exception to what any reasonable person would regard as being perfectly innocent. Fortunately they are in the minority, but *reasonable* people are not, and you should tailor your material to suit their standards of acceptability. If in doubt, leave it out.

7. Don't arrive late or dressed incorrectly. Arriving late puts everyone on edge and the wrong clothes put you at a disadvantage before you open your mouth. Try to blend with the surroundings. If you feel confident and relaxed, you'll communicate this to your audience soon enough.

8. Don't stop in the middle of a speech if you think it isn't going very well. The audience may respond differently to the way you anticipated, but persevere. Carry on in an unflustered way and they won't notice that anything is amiss. At all costs complete the speech, even it it means cutting it short and delivering your conclusion ahead of time. At least that will give it a semblance of unity and only you will know that any modification had to be made.

9. Don't tire yourself out before you start. Speaking in public, even if only for a five-minute vote of thanks, is an exhausting experience. It is pointless staying up late the night before putting the last touches to your speech, by the time you come to deliver it, you probably won't be in a fit state to give of your best as a result. In order to have the necessary edge you need to keep your reserves of mental and physical energy well topped up.

10. Don't go on for too long. Even if you're obviously bringing the house down, don't overstay your welcome. Your speech will benefit from being brief. Remember, a speech can never be too short, only too long.

H ELP!

However well you prepare yourself for an after-dinner speech there will be times when things don't go according to plan. You may be unlucky enough to be interrupted by a heckler; you may even have to respond to a disaster like a power cut; you may have to respond to a slip of the tongue of your own making. Whatever situation you find yourself in, try not to panic. All may not be lost.

In this section I'd like to offer some tips to help you through those nerve-wracking moments after you've realized that the floor isn't going to open up and swallow you. Few after-dinner speakers escape without the occasional mishap at some time in their speaking career, so you won't be alone if you find yourself suddenly thrown from your carefully planned and intricately rehearsed delivery. As Hamlet says, admittedly in rather different circumstances, 'the readiness is all.'

Hecklers

Unless you feel totally confident about making spontaneous and stinging ripostes, it's wisest to ignore hecklers. If a sudden flash of inspiration delivers the very retort you need to silence a heckler, use it. Certain politicians have established notable reputations for their quick-witted dismissal of hecklers at the hustings. To a man who shouted, 'I'd rather vote for the devil than John Wilkes,' Wilkes calmly answered, 'And if your friend is not standing?' Few speakers have the ability to hit back as tellingly as that and if you haven't a suitable rejoinder, press on with your speech and leave the heckler to be silenced by his neighbours who he'll be annoying as much.

Experienced speakers sometimes have a clutch of favourite put-downs that they use to stifle persistent heckling, but it takes practice for a retort to carry enough weight to silence someone who's determined to get you rattled. Lord Mancroft was one such speaker who demonstrated his skill as a speaker by telling a man who kept interrupting one of his speeches very loudly: 'A man with your intelligence should have a voice to match.'

The danger in responding to hecklers is that you may encourage them still further. There's the story of one speaker who complained to his chairman that there was so much interruption that he couldn't hear himself speak. 'Don't worry,' shouted a voice from the audience, 'you're not missing much.' The fact is that hecklers, particularly where after-dinner speakers are concerned, are pretty thin on the ground. Providing you do nothing to stimulate heckling there is very little likelihood of being interrupted.

One invitation to heckle that you can certainly take steps to avoid is speaking for too long. If you are running over time and your audience is showing signs of restlessness, you may well deserve the occasional shout of complaint. One MP, entering the twentieth minute of what he had promised would only be a 'short' speech, told his audience, 'I not only speak for you, but for the generations as yet unborn,' which earned him the reply, 'If you

don't speed up, they'll be here before you've finished.'
With the right preparation this pitfall can and should be
avoided.

Coping with Calamities
The unexpected can happen even at the best organized
dinners. The lights might fail; someone might drop a stack
of plates on the way to the kitchen; the microphone might
start squealing; you might carelessly knock over your glass
of water. The important point to remember with these and
similar events is that you shouldn't ignore them and
soldier on as if nothing had happened. Everyone else will
be just as aware as you that something has gone wrong,
but as the speaker it's your responsibility to acknowledge
the fact and then return to your speech calmly and confidently unless it is totally impractical.

An amusing aside about a tray of smashed glasses ('So
that's what they meant by trying to break the ice') or if you
do spill your glass of water ('I'm terribly sorry, for a
moment I thought my trousers were on fire') will relieve
any tension that might have built up and should allow you
to get back to your speech while the audience have a
chuckle.

Quick-witted speakers can often use the unexpected to
their advantage. When Lord Mountbatten was speaking
on one occasion, one of the Marine guard of honour
standing behind him suddenly passed out and fainted
across the table. Without even looking at the man,
Mountbatten remarked, 'You will notice that one of the
admirable qualities the Marines possess is the ability to
faint at attention.'

Equally inspired is the story of the American professor
who had the misfortune to take a seat that had recently
been given a fresh coat of varnish. As he rose to speak at

the end of the dinner, he found that his chair rose with him. Having eventually prized himself free, he turned to his audience and began, 'Ladies and gentlemen, I had hoped to bring you this evening a plain and unvarnished tale, but circumstances make it impossible for me to fulfil my intentions.' If you wanted a pre-arranged stunt to open a speech you couldn't wish for anything better, but his obvious spontaneity gave his opening a freshness that no contrivance could capture.

Personal Slip-ups

Don't be lulled into thinking that these will never happen to you; try to avoid them, but never become complacent. We all make innocent slips of the tongue and if you apologize gracefully and continue with your speech, whatever you said will probably have been forgotten by the time you come to your closing remarks. Trying to bluff your way through an obvious *faux pas,* or pretending that you didn't say it is unlikely to succeed and you'll probably have the audience laughing their heads off anyway. Take the man who introduced his guests of honour with these words: 'Let me first give you a few biological details about the Duke and Duchess of Bedford,' only to stammer out a moment later, 'I mean biographical.' Or there is Gerald Ford proposing a toast to Anwar Sadat at a White House dinner and asking the others present to raise their glasses to 'The President of Israel . . . er, Egypt.' Neither had any option but to correct the mistake and try to retrieve their dignity.

You might care to inject a little elegant humour into your own predicament by quoting a famous example, like those above, or even resorting to verse, like the example below, as a means of acknowledging your error but making amends for it at the same time.

HELP!

'Shiver me timbers,' said Nelson to Emma,
'I don't mind admitting I'm in a dilemma.

Though Cockburn's a port far-famed and renowned
When I try to pronounce it, my tongue runs aground.'

Lady E's smile shows a cute little dimple
And she says 'My dear Nelson, it's really quite simple.

The 'O' is as long as a midsummer day
And you turn your blind eye to the C and the K.'

Perhaps the most serious threat to any after-dinner speaker is finding that his speech isn't going down well with the audience. Panic can sometimes lead speakers into including unprepared material, but this is a dangerous course and can often be counter-productive. It's frequently far safer to stick to your planned speech, shortening it perhaps, but bringing it to an orderly and clear-cut conclusion before sitting down. In that way you won't give the impression of having been panicked into a sudden and unconvincing ending.

Keep your head when faced with the unexpected and you stand a far greater chance of winning through than you will by getting flustered and possibly making matters worse.

I N SICKNESS AND IN HEALTH

As I mentioned in the Introduction, the sections that follow (excepting the final three) contain a variety of source material that you might find useful in formulating a speech of your own. Each section covers a different topic and within each the material is broadly sub-divided into three categories: stories and anecdotes, jokes, and quotations.

At the head of the list comes a subject of universal interest and one that finds its way into so many strands of our lives, namely our state of health and the medical profession who have the often unwelcome task of keeping us going.

Medical humour can have a very wide appeal. Most of your audience are likely to have visited a doctor in the not too distant past; some may have spent time in hospital; and others may themselves be members of the profession. Used tactfully and with good humour, medical material will often strike a common chord with an audience. As long as you avoid tasteless jokes about serious illness and steer well clear of other subjects that could cause offence you may find a medical line an entertaining one to take, particularly in the early stages of a speech when the audience are still adjusting to you and a human touch can help put them at ease.

Stories
Benjamin Disraeli was able to use what he must have regarded as universal hypochondria to his social advantage as was made evident when he once confided: 'When I meet someone whose name I cannot remember, I allow the conversation to proceed for approximately two minutes. If it is still a hopeless case, I always change the subject with, "And how is the old complaint?" '

For several years an old soldier had been convinced that he was about to suffer a debilitating stroke. One night, while he was enjoying a quiet game of draughts with a much younger officer, he suddenly became very agitated. 'It's happened at last,' he cried.
'I'm paralysed all down my right side.'
'Are you sure, sir?' asked his junior.
'Certain of it,' said the old man. 'I've been pinching my leg throughout his game and I haven't felt a thing.'
'Actually, sir, it's my leg you've been pinching. I wondered what was going on.'

The Victorian artist James Whistler was the proud owner of a poodle on which he doted. One day the dog developed a throat infection and its owner, by-passing orthodox veterinary practice, went straight to the country's leading ear, nose and throat specialist, Sir Morell Mackenzie. Sir Morell didn't take kindly to being asked to treat an animal, but he conducted a routine examination and gave Whistler a prescription. The next day Whistler got an urgent

53

message from Sir Morell asking him to call on him. Suspecting that this might mean a development in his poodle's condition, he hurried to the doctor's house where Sir Morell greeted him gravely and said: 'Thank you for coming so promptly, Whistler. I wanted to consult you about having my front door painted.'

A retired skin specialist was asked late in life why he had chosen to follow this branch of medicine, and replied: 'The answer is perfectly simple. My patients never get me out of bed at night; they never die of the complaint; and they never recover.'

Jokes

A patient told his doctor that he always had a terrible pain in his chest whenever he raised his arm.
'Well, stop raising it then,' the doctor told him.

Two psychiatrists passed in a hospital corridor and one said to his colleague: 'You're feeling good, how am I?'

A woman went to see a psychiatrist with worries about her state of mind and spent twenty minutes telling him her life story. She told him about her childhood, her emotional life, her work, what she ate, her dreams, even where she went for her holidays. When the doctor had a chance to get a word in he said to her: 'As far as I can see, there's absolutely nothing wrong with you. In fact you seem quite able to cope with life. All in all I'd say you were as normal as I am.'

'But doctor,' said the woman, 'what about those butterflies? They're crawling all over me. I can't stand it any longer!'

'For crying out loud!' yelled the psychiatrist, backing away, 'don't flick them all over me.'

A patient who wanted to express his thanks in a tangible way to his doctor asked if he was fond of shellfish.

'I wouldn't say I was fond of them,' replied the doctor, 'but I'm very grateful to them.'

A doctor who presented his bill to the executor of a recently deceased patient asked whether it had to be sworn to.

'That will not be necessary,' he was told. 'My late client's death is sufficient evidence that you attended him professionally.'

Two women were discussing a mutual friend who had recently begun visiting a psychiatrist.

'Is she being treated because she's highly strung?' asked one.

'Heavens, no,' said her companion. 'With all her money she's rich enough to be psychoneurotic.'

Quotations

The art of medicine consists of amusing the patient while nature takes care of the disease. *Voltaire*

The pen is mightier than the sword! The case for prescriptions rather than surgery. *Marvin Litman*

There are worse occupations in this world than feeling a woman's pulse. *Laurence Sterne*

IN SICKNESS AND IN HEALTH ───────────────

A neurotic is the man who builds a castle in the air. A psychotic is the man who lives in it. And a psychiatrist is the man who collects the rent. *Anonymous*

A vasectomy is never having to say you're sorry. *Rubin Carson*

Psychiatry's chief contribution to philosophy is the discovery that the toilet is the seat of the soul. *Alexander Chase*

J OBS FOR THE BOYS

Many after-dinner speeches are associated in one way or another with the world of work. They might form part of a retirement dinner, they might celebrate a company success; they might simply be part of the annual Christmas dinner. Whatever they are, after-dinner speeches associated with your own or other people's places of work should appeal to an audience if they can relate to them by identifying with the people or events you mention.

Companies and offices frequently have their own collections of stories and anecdotes. As mentioned earlier, amusing episodes in a colleague's career can often form an entertaining backbone to a speech about him. In the same way a speech to an audience employed in a specific type of work will be all the more appealing if it contains some reference to the type of work they do themselves.

Here you'll find a few of the items connected with the world of work that have amused me, and may inspire you.

Stories
The Post Office handle some very strange correspondence especially at Christmas. At most sorting-offices they open the mail addressed to Father Christmas. One year a postman found a letter from

a pensioner asking for £5 to give himself a Christmas treat. All the men were very touched by the request, and decided to make a collection for the old man. Altogether they collected £3.54, which was made up to £4 by the office foreman. Four pound notes were duly sent off to the pensioner with a note saying, 'All the best from Santa Claus.' A couple of days later, there was another note from the old man: 'Dear Father Christmas, thank you so much for the money — it will come in very useful. By the way, I reckon those miserly sods down at the Post Office have nicked one of the notes.'

A Managing Director, looking for new ideas to

improve his company's performance, decided to consult his men. He pinned a notice up in the canteen which read: 'When I come down to the shop floor I like to see everyone happily getting on with their work. Anyone who has any suggestions as to how this may be brought about more efficiently, please place them in the box below.'

The next day, a piece of paper lay all alone in the box. It read: 'Take the rubber heels off your shoes.'

The president of an association of professional men posed the question at one of their regular dinners: 'Which profession among those represented here can claim to be the oldest?'

While the Cockburn's port was being passed round the table, a surgeon rose to his feet and said:

'When God created Eve, he took a rib from Adam knowing that a surgeon's skill would be needed.'

An architect then got up to make his claim:

'In order to restore order out of Chaos, God must have required the skills of an architect.'

At this, a Civil Servant jumped up and demanded:

'Ah yes, but who created Chaos?'

Professional mistakes can sometimes lead to unfortunate consequences. A man from Barnsley who had just lost his wife asked a local monumental mason to make a headstone with the words: 'She was thine.' When the man went to visit his wife's grave, he saw that a mistake had been made. The stone read: 'She was thin.' When he got home, he rang the mason and complained, 'You've left off the "E". ' The mason offered his deepest apologies, and promised he would put it right as soon as possible.

When the man returned to the cemetery the following week, the message on the headstone now read: ' 'E SHE WAS THIN.'

Jokes

A senior executive, who as a young salesman had made quite a reputation for himself with his phenomenal record, told a group of new sales recruits: 'I owe my success to the first seven words which I invariably said when a woman opened the door, "Miss, may I speak to your mother?" '

A Wall Street broker was taken to hospital with a fever and between periods of unconsciousness overheard one of the nurses saying: 'Temperature today, 102.'
Opening his eyes, the broker looked at her and said wearily: 'When it reaches 102½, sell.'

A manager who noticed that all the letters he had dictated to his secretary contained mistakes caught up with the girl a she was leaving the office in the evening and said: 'What's wrong with you, don't you know the Queen's English?'
'Of course I do,' the girl replied indignantly. 'Otherwise she wouldn't be our queen, would she?'

A busy executive who had condescended to see a young life insurance salesman told him: 'You have reason to feel pleased with yourself, young man. I've refused to see six insurance men today.'
'I know, sir,' said the salesman, 'I'm them.'

A foreman came across one of the men in a flour mill
60

carrying just one sack of flour while everyone else was carrying two. When he was asked to explain this the worker replied: 'That's because the others are too lazy to make two trips, like I do.'

Quotations

If you don't want to work you have to work to earn enough money so that you won't have to work. *Ogden Nash*

Work expands to fill the time available for its completion. *C. Northcote Parkinson*

Anyone can do any amount of work provided it isn't the work he is supposed to be doing at the moment. *Robert Benchley*

All work and no play makes Jack a dull boy — and Jill a wealthy widow. *Evan Esar*

Corporation: An ingenious device for obtaining individual profit without individual responsibility. *Ambrose Bierce*

If all the efficiency experts in the world were laid end to end — I'd be in favour of it. *Al Diamond*

K INDLY LEAVE THE STAGE

As a form of entertainment itself, after-dinner speaking can draw a lot of valuable material from show business and the world of professional entertainment. The stage, the cinema, radio and television are rich repositories of humorous anecdotes, memorable quotations and witty retorts. Show business is frequently a common territory shared by speaker and audience who are both likely to be familiar with popular films, plays and radio and television programmes. Stories and comments featuring actors and other show business personalities in the public eye can be drawn on to illustrate a point and add colour to many speeches.

Dozens of books have been filled with theatre anecdotes; jokes about the world of entertainment are legion, and dictionaries of quotations carry almost all the memorable comments and observations from the world of entertainment. Here I can only give an indication of the range of material available. It's a source well worth tapping.

Stories
A reporter once asked W. C. Fields whether he had experienced any side-effects from his alcoholism

since coming to Hollywood. 'I don't know,' replied Fields. 'It's difficult to tell where the D.T.'s stop and Hollywood begins.'

The story (no doubt apochryphal) is told that when Sam Goldwyn noticed how well Radclyffe Hall's book *The Well of Loneliness* was selling, he decided he wanted to buy the film rights. When the news got round the studio, one of his assistants rushed to his office.

63

'You won't be able to film that book,' he advised breathlessly.
'It's all about lesbians.'
'No problem,' replied Goldwyn calmly, 'where the book's got Lesbians we'll use Austrians.'

When Katherine Hepburn first met her co-star in so many successful films, Spencer Tracy, there was a feeling of nervous apprehension in the air. On being introduced to her leading man, Miss Hepburn observed tartly:
'I see I'm a little tall for you, Mr Tracy.'
To which Spencer Tracy immediately replied:
'Never mind, Miss Hepburn. I'll soon cut you down to size.'

When a famous Hollywood producer rang Bernard Shaw to try and secure the film rights to some of his plays, he found him a tough bargainer. In an endeavour to reduce Shaw's uncompromising terms, the producer decided to appeal to his conscience as an artist.
'Look at it like this, Mr Shaw. Millions of people who have never had the pleasure of seeing one of your plays will at last get the chance to see them. You'd be making a great contribution to Art.'
'The trouble is this,' replied Shaw. 'You think only of Art, while I think only of money.'

Noel Coward was once having an awful time during the rehearsals for the touring production of *The Young Idea*. His leading lady insisted on ruining the whole rhythm of the scene by dwelling too long on each of her lines. When Coward started ticking her off, the actress lost her temper and shouted at him: 'If you carry on like that, I'll throw something at you.' 'Then you might start with my cues?' replied Coward

John Barrymore used to tell this story about the hurly-burly of repertory theatre in the 1920s. Like most companies, his used to stage a great many different plays in a given season, making it almost impossible not to make the occasional slip. During a scene one evening, Barrymore suddenly realized that he didn't know his next line. Improvising like mad, he wandered nonchalantly over to the wings and whispered to the director who he'd noticed standing just off-stage:
'What's the line, what's the line?'
The director looked at him wearily, and replied, 'What's the play?'

The writer Keith Waterhouse tells a funny story about what might be called the lower end of the 'Profession'. A director, a little the worse for drink, was sitting in a nightclub when he saw what he thought was a familiar face. He called its owner over to this table and proceeded to praise him for a recent performance. The actor quickly pointed out that he hadn't been in that particular play
'Oh, well, it must have been in *Macbeth* at the Old Vic,' persisted the director.
Once again the actor said he hadn't appeared in that play either.
'What was it then?' asked the director straining to remember. 'You see I remember being extremely impressed with your performance.'

The actor explained to him that he had actually been out of work for nearly a year, and that the only job he had at the time was in the Food Hall in Harrods.

The director's eyes lit up. 'That's it,' he said with relief.

'That's where I've seen you. And you were really very good, very good indeed!'

Jokes

A young actor, determined to break into the world of films, even though he had been turned down a number of times by the same company, decided to make one final effort. He went to see the casting director and said: 'This is your last chance to have me in one of your pictures. Let me tell you, there are lots of companies after me.'

The director looked interested, though sceptical, and asked the young man, 'Which companies exactly?'

'Well, there's the gas company, the electricity company, the telephone company, the furniture company . . .'

Luckily the director had a sense of humour, and the actor got his job.

A variety artist who took exception to going on stage right after a troop of performing monkeys complained to the show's director: 'Look, I don't think it's right that I should go out there right after the chimps.'

'You've got a point,' the director told him, 'they might think it's an encore.'

A man walked into a barber's shop a few years ago and asked for a Tony Curtis haircut. The barber thought for a while, and then settled down enthusiastically into the job. After a few minutes he had managed to shave the customer's head completely bare. The man was furious.

'Don't you know who Tony Curtis is?' he shouted.

'Of course I do,' replied the barber. 'I watch *Kojak* every week.'

A film salesman with the job of selling Hollywood's latest offerings in South America offered the latest Clark Gable film to a cinema owner in a remote part of Venezuela only to be told: 'Clark Gable is dead. You recall the film *Parnell?*'

'I sure do. It was a box-office winner.'

'Yes, senor, but the Gable he die in it '

'Yeah, but that was only . . .'

'I try to show another Gable film after that. What happen? I have a riot. My clients see the Gable die in one picture. Can a man not believe his own eyes? So far as this village knows, the Gable — he is dead.'

Quotations

The art of acting consists of keeping people from coughing. *Sir Ralph Richardson.*

An actor's a guy who, if you ain't talking about him, ain't listening. *Marlon Brando*

Men go to the theatre to forget; women, to remember *George Jean Nathan*

I had all the schooling an actress needs. That is, I learned to write enough to sign contracts. *Hermione Gingold*

I find television very educating. Every time somebody turns on the set I go into the other room and read a book. *Groucho Marx*

When you're a young man, Macbeth is a character part. When you're older, it's a straight part. *Lord Olivier*

LOVERS' TALK

It used to be said that a speaker had only to get to his feet and announce: 'I am a married man' to bring the house down. The days of that sort of chauvinism are happily behind us, but speakers who are able to personalize what they say are going to win over their audiences far sooner than those who don't. Affairs of the heart, whether as suitor or spouse, and the day-to-day ups and downs of married life nearly always ring true if handled good humouredly, especially if you make use of original material taken from your own experiences.

The examples given here illustrate some memorable attitudes to the relationship between men and women which might be of use in conjunction with material of your own.

Stories
Dr Johnson, who seemed to harbour a permanent grudge against the opposite sex, had this to say about a man who married for a second time immediately after the death of his first wife: 'His conduct was a triumph of hope over experience.'

One of the things many couples find difficult is

coming to terms with their partner's past affairs. Samuel Foote was discussing the forthcoming marriage of a lady friend with a group of fellow actors one evening. The entire company was aware that she had enjoyed an energetic and wide-ranging love life.

'Did you know,' remarked one of the group, 'She has made a full confession about her past to her husband?'

'All those affairs?' asked another. 'What honesty she must have had, what courage!'

'Yes,' interjected Foote, 'but what a memory!'

The French politician Talleyrand once described the career of a notorious woman-about-town with the comment: 'In order to avoid the scandal of coquetry, Madame always yields easily.'

When a 74-year-old woman filed a divorce suit against her 86-year-old husband, the judge asked how long they had been married. She replied, 'Fifty-five years.'

'So why are you asking for a divorce after all this time?' he enquired.

'Enough is enough,' the woman said.

An Archbishop, attending a confirmation ceremony in a small town, heard the vicar ask a nervous little girl to define the state of matrimony.

'It's a time of awful torment which some of us must undergo before we are allowed to enter a better world,' she replied.

'No, my child,' corrected the vicar, 'that is not a definition of matrimony, but of Purgatory.'

70

'Let the child be,' interrupted the Archbishop. 'Perhaps she has been allowed to see the light.'

Jokes

A husband, anxious to get into his wife's good books after an argument, decided to take her out for a romantic evening. They went to the theatre, followed by a lovely meal and a walk by the river. By the time they arrived home, all was well.

'Thank you for a beautiful evening, darling,' she said as they walked through the door.

'But it's not over yet,' he replied. 'How about a delicious glass of Cockburn's port to round the evening off?'

She agreed, and as she raised the glass to her lips, he offered her two small white tablets.

'Aren't these aspirins?' she asked.

'Yes they are.'

'But I haven't got a headache, darling,' she said.

'Right,' said her husband, 'Let's go to bed!'

'I've really managed to save some money this month, darling,' a young wife told her husband.

'Wonderful! It wasn't that hard I bet.'

'Not at all. I left the house-keeping bills for you to pay instead.'

A woman appeared in a police station in a very distraught state and told the duty-officer that her husband had disappeared.

'This is his picture. Please find him,' she implored. The policeman took a look at the photograph and asked: 'Why?'

A couple who eloped after a whirlwind romance only started to get to know each other on their honeymoon. After a few days the husband discovered to his amazement that his bride was a snake-charmer. Slightly stunned by this he asked with air of reproach: 'Why on earth didn't you tell me?'

'Because you never asked,' she replied.

Quotations

It begins as you sink into his arms, and ends with your arms in the sink. *Anonymous graffiti*

A kiss is a course procedure, cunningly devised, for the mutual stoppage of speech at a moment when words are superfluous. *Oliver Herford*

He married an Anglo-Indian widow, and soon after published a pamphlet in favour of suttee. *George Meredith*

The most difficult year of marriage is the one you're in. *Franklin P. Jones*

Marriage — a community consisting of a master, a mistress, and two slaves — making in all two. *Ambrose Bierce*

Marriage is the deep, deep peace of the double bed after the hurly-burly of the chaise longue. *Mrs Patrick Campbell*

No matter how happily a woman may be married, it always pleases her to discover that there is a nice man who wishes she were not. *H. L. Mencken*

LOVERS TALK ───────────────────

The great secret of successful marriage is to treat all disasters as incidents and none of the incidents as disasters. *Harold Nicholson*

Mess Dress

A good many audiences will have had some experience of life in the forces, either on active service or by courtesy of

HELL'S ANGELS 12ᵀᴴ CHAPTER

When I was asked to speak at a dinner given by military enthusiasts I thought.....

conscription. Plenty of others will be familiar with vignettes of service life from stereotyped senior officers to the argot of the ranks, thanks to television and the cinema. After-dinner material with a gentle military flavour is often a beguiling means of bridging a generation gap and examples drawn from service life can often be used to point up some of the more entertaining foibles of human nature.

Stories

The Duke of Wellington was a notoriously blunt speaker irrespective of who he was talking to. On one occasion, George IV was bragging to the general about his exploits as a young cavalry officer. Wellington made no comment until the King pointed to a precipitous hill a few hundred yards away, and boasted:

'I remember that hill well. I once galloped down it at the head of my regiment.'

Wellington, raising an eyebrow ever so slightly, turned to him and said, 'Rather steep, sir.'

A newspaper report a few years ago talked of the concern in the Coldstream Guards over the number of men fainting while on parade, especially at the Trooping of the Colour. As a result an order was given that on the night before large, public parades, single men below the rank of sergeant were to be confined; while married men had to move out of their normal quarters and into those occupied by bachelors.

Field Marshall Montgomery, like many comman-ders during the Second World War, grew to appreciate the value of good public relations. When a *Daily Mirror* reporter in Yorkshire wrote to him with a suggested promotion he was quick to respond. The reporter, Ronald Bedford, had heard about a hen called Emma that belonged to a soldier serving under Monty. Lance Corporal Walsh kept Emma in his tank and his parents wrote to their local paper in Yorkshire with a suggestion that she be made a sergeant. Monty went one better and immediately promoted Emma to the rank of sergeant-major.

As recently as 1975 the British Army still relied on animal transport. A review of defence expenditure that year concluded that the combined efforts of the helicopter and the four-wheeled drive vehicle (which had been in existence for the best part of thirty years) had finally rendered the mule redundant, and at the end of the year the No. 414 Pack Transport Troop Royal Corps of Transport (Hong Kong) unsaddled for the last time.

During the war of 1812 between Britain and the USA, Admiral George Cockburn led an incendiary party against the offices of the *National Intelligencer* when the British burned down Washington. During the course of the raid he commanded his men to melt down all the *c*'s in the print room 'so that later they can't abuse my name.' (He was one Cockburn who obviously appreciated the difficulties his name could cause.)

Jokes
Two girls who hadn't seen each other since they left

school met for lunch one day at the Ritz. The conversation soon turned to men:

'Virginia, I've heard that you have become engaged to an army chappie,' one of them said.

'That's right, darling. He's called Captain Tarquin Villiers of the First African Rifles.'

'Oh, aren't they coloured?'

'Not completely — only the Privates.'

'Goodness gracious! How exotic.'

A young private was at a party when he caught sight of his commanding officer across the room. He turned to the pretty girl beside him and said:

'Look at that miserable old devil over there, he's the meanest man in the regiment.'

'Do you know who I am?' replied the girl. 'I'm that miserable old devil's daughter.'

'Really? Do you know who I am?' asked the soldier.

'No.'

'Thank God for that!'

One Allied prisoner-of-war who appealed for assistance from the French Resistance found himself entrusted to a local circus owner. The owner decided that it would be too dangerous simply to disguise the prisoner as one of his employees. Instead he proposed that he wear the skin of one of the gorillas who had died recently. Unhappy, but with no choice, the prisoner agreed.

As the circus travelled across the country, the 'gorilla' was called on to perform now and again, which he did to the best of his ability. One night, while he was resting in his cage, he noticed that the bars of the adjoining cage had come loose.

Suddenly he realised that the lion from the neighbouring cage had slipped into his one. As the lion moved towards him, the 'gorilla' became panic-sticken and started shouting for help.

'Be quiet, you idiot,' said the lion. 'You aren't the only prisoner-of-war around here, you know.'

An elderly woman helping to nurse the wounded returning from the D-Day beaches bent solicitously over a soldier whose head was swathed in bandages and asked: 'Have you been wounded in the head, my boy?'

'No lady,' said the soldier, 'I was shot in the foot but the bandages slipped up.'

While they were sailing back to port after taking part in anti-submarine exercises, the captain of a British destroyer sent a signal to his fellow commander on board the submarine that had been acting as their target, asking if he ever got fed up sitting on the bottom having explosives dropped on him. The reply came back:

'Hebrews 13:8'.

The ship's bible was fetched and the reference found. It read: 'Jesus Christ the same yesterday, and today, and forever.'

A sailor who was asked how he had spent his pay replied: 'Some went on drink, some on women and the rest I squandered.'

A young subaltern fresh from Sandhurst appeared before his company for the first time and was greeted by mutterings about his youth and obvious inexperience. During his brief inspection a voice from the rear called out: 'And a little child shall lead them.' The lieutenant didn't appear to notice this remark and completed his round. The following day an order was pinned to the company's notice board announcing that all ranks would undertake a twenty-mile march with full packs. At the bottom of the order was the line: 'And a little child shall lead them . . . on a damned big horse.'

Quotations

Some are born great, some achieve greatness, and others have it pinned on them. *George Ade*

War is too important to leave to the generals. *Georges Clemenceau*

Military intelligence is a contradiction in terms. *Groucho Marx*

We may not be the greatest at winning Winter Olympics but at least we can carry our bloody flag properly. *Squadron Leader Mike Freeman (British bobsleigher in 1972).*

NOT QUITE NICE

Samuel Butler once said: 'Life is like playing a violin solo in public and learning the instrument as one goes along.' If your life is full of music, it's inevitable that you'll play a wrong note now and again and that others will secretly relish your discomfort. The little slips and the major *faux pas* we all commit by accident are the stuff on which so much humour is based. 'There but for the grace of God go I', we say to ourselves revelling in someone else's embarrassment in the certain knowledge that our next banana skin is only round the corner.

After-dinner speaking is above all a social activity and material drawn from social life fits easily and naturally into the tenor of many after-dinner speeches. It's human and natural too. If you can bear to be honest in public there are probably a few skeletons in your own social wardrobe that would greatly amuse your audience as well. The items below give you a flavour of the sort of material which often goes down well in the right environment.

Stories

At a literary luncheon some years ago, the guest speaker was forced to withdraw after suffering a mild nervous breakdown a few weeks before the event. Though a substitute had been arranged, the news came through at the last minute that the original speaker intended to turn up after all.

When the organizer arrived, he noticed that his distinguished guest was already deep in conversation with an elderly lady. As he walked over to greet the man, the lady, whom he knew quite well, turned to him and said:

'Darling, I've just been explaining to this charming gentleman how our main speaker has gone off his rocker.'

The blunders are not always verbal. The Archbishop of York was guest of honour once at a large and impressive dinner in the City. Unfortunately, as the first course was being served, one of the waiters slipped and deposited a bowl of soup in the illustrious clergyman's lap. The Archbishop looked despairingly around the table and said: 'Is there any layman present who will be good enough to express my feelings?'

Exactly the same thing happened to the actress Beatrice Lillie when she was once a guest at Buckingham Palace. For a moment a dreadful silence descended as everyone glared at the unfortunate waiter until Miss Lillie saved the day by telling him with mock anger: 'Never darken my Dior again.'

Sir Thomas Beecham was once conducting the Halle Orchestra in Manchester, and feeling a little weary, he decided to go straight back to his hotel after the performance. Entering the lobby, he noticed a lady sitting by the lift. Though he could not put a name to her face, he recognized her immediately, and realised that he could not avoid talking to her as he made his way to his room.

'Good evening, madam,' he said, pausing at the lift. 'I hope you enjoyed the concert.'

They chatted for a moment or two, during which Sir Thomas managed to conceal his ignorance of who the lady was. As he was about to take his leave he remembered that she had a brother, and politely enquired:

'And how is your brother?'

'He's very well thank you, Sir Thomas.'

'And what is he doing at the moment?'

'He is still king.'

Brian Johnston was commentating once on a Test Match between England and West Indies. England were batting at the time, with Peter Willey facing the fast bowler Michael Holding. As Holding came in to bowl, Brian Johnston told his listeners:

'The bowler's Holding, the batsman's Willey.'

Jokes

A couple were entertaining a large house party in their sumptuous country home. On the first night they provided their guests with a lavish dinner and then offered the full range of amusements the house afforded. As the evening wore on, the hostess offered to show the young daughter of one of her friends around. On entering one of the drawing-rooms, she was horrified to discover two of her guests cavorting naked in front of the fire. 'Mending the hearth-rug — how thoughtful,' she observed, ushering the child out again.

A best man who had consumed vast amounts of 'vino collapso' during the course of a reception was a little the worse for wear by the time the party in the evening arrived. As he was circulating among the guests, he suddenly overheard a conversation about the merits of holidaying in Wales and unable to stop himself offering an opinion, blurted out: 'There are only two worthwhile things which have come from Wales — rugby players and prostitutes.' Hearing this, a huge man walked up and prodded him menacingly on the shoulder, saying: 'My wife was born and bred in Wales.' The best man looked at this fuming giant for a few seconds before asking: 'Oh really, and what position did she play?'

A guest who had more than outstayed his welcome eventually rose to leave and thanked his host and hostess, saying: 'I did enjoy myself, I hope I haven't kept you up too late.'
'Not at all,' the husband replied. 'We would be getting up soon anyway.'

A hostess sitting at the opposite end of the table to a great friend of hers jotted a note and asked the butler to deliver it to her discreetly. Unfortunately the lady couldn't read it without her glasses and asked the man on her left what it said. 'It reads,' he began, 'Be a dear and please try to liven up the man on your left. He's a terrible bore but do talk to him.'

Quotations

Tact is the ability to describe others as they see themselves. *Abraham Lincolm*

In the battle of existence, talent is the punch; tact is the clever footwork. *Wilson Mizner*

Behaviour: Conduct, as determined, not by principle, but by breeding. *Ambrose Bierce*

There are people whom one should like very well to drop, but would not wish to be dropped by. *Dr Johnson*

You are ushered in according to your dress; shown out according to your brain. *Yiddish proverb*

Etiquette can be at the same time a means of approaching people and of staying clear of them. *David Riesman*

ORDER, ORDER

The world of politics has produced some of the wittiest after-dinner speakers. It has also been the setting for many memorable anecdotes and equally celebrated quotations. Contemporary politicians may sometimes seem to lack the verbal and mental dexterity of their predecessors (although there are notable exceptions) but as political life is part and parcel of our own lives today, with so much coverage on radio and television, as well as in the press, the antics of government and politicians invariably appeal to a wide range of audiences.

Stories
Harold Wilson, during his time as Leader of the Opposition, took great delight in rubbing the salt in the Conservative government's wounds. He once said in Parliament: 'Everytime Mr Macmillan returns from abroad, Mr Butler goes to the airport and grips him warmly by the throat.'

Sir Geoffrey Howe, who was in Opposition at the time, made a speech condemning the Labour government's economic policy. As Chancellor of the Exchequer, it was Denis Healey's job to reply.

He rose to his feet and congratulated Sir Geoffrey on his speech, saying that he felt as if he had been 'savaged by a dead sheep.'

A leading member of the Tory party was delivering a speech one day in the House of Commons, when

Sir Winston Churchill began to shake his head in disagreement from the back-benches. Noticing this, the Minister commented:
'I see that my honourable colleague is shaking his head. May I remind him that I am merely expressing my own opinion.'
'Mr Speaker,' replied Churchill, 'may I remind the Minister that I am merely shaking my own head.'

On one occasion George Bernard Shaw sent Churchill two tickets for the first night of his new play in the West End. He also enclosed a note: 'Please find enclosed two tickets — one for yourself and one for a friend, if you have one.'
Churchill returned the tickets to Shaw enclosing a little note of his own which read: 'I regret that I will not be able to attend the first night of your new play. Perhaps I could have a couple of tickets for the second night, if you have one?'

Benjamin Disraeli, who once referred to Gladstone as a man without a 'single redeeming feature,' was asked on another occasion to distinguish between a 'calamity' and a 'misfortune'.
'It would be a misfortune,' he replied. 'if Mr Gladstone were to slip and fall into the River Thames. However it would be a calamity if someone were to fish him out.'

When Robert Menzies was sworn in as Prime Minister of Australia, the world's press and television were on hand to ask questions. One reporter asked him bluntly:
'Will you be consulting the powerful interests which

support and control your government when you
come to choose a Cabinet?' A buzz of anticipation
went round the press conference but the Prime
Minister calmly replied:
'Please, can we keep my wife's name out of this.'

Jokes
An MP who observed one of his fellows deep in
prayer asked him afterwards if he was praying for
the House.
'No,' his friend told him, 'I take a look at the House
and pray for the country.'

Politics has been described as a process in which
one man gets up and says nothing. Nobody listens
and then everyone starts disagreeing.

A young peer asked one of his seniors to advise him
how he might best practice his oratory to gain the
ear of the Upper House.
'Is there a graveyard near your home?' asked the
older man.
'There is.'
'Then I suggest you take a stroll there every
morning and practise on the tombstones.'

In an effort to outline the principal political doctrines
of the twentieth century the following list was drawn
up and is worth considering:
CAPITALISM — You possess two cows; you sell one
and buy a bull.
SOCIALISM — You possess two cows; you give one of
them to your neighbour.
COMMUNISM — You possess two cows; the
88

government takes both of them away, but provides you with milk.

FACISM — You possess two cows; the government takes both of them away, and sells you the milk.

NAZISM — You possess two cows; the government takes both of them away, and shoots you.

THE COMMON MARKET — You possess two cows; the government takes both of them away, shoots one of them, milks the other, and pours it all down the drain.

Quotations

I never vote for the best candidate, I vote for the one who will do the least harm. *Franklin K. Dane*

There are only two kinds of government — the good and the bad. The good has never yet existed. The bad operates on the principle of transferring the property of its opponents into the pockets of its supporters. *Dean Inge*

A Conservative is someone who will not look at the new moon, out of respect for that ancient institution, the old one. *Douglas Jerrold*

The nation is prosperous on the whole, but how much prosperity is there in a hole? *Will Rogers*

Nothing is so admirable in politics as a short memory. *J. K. Galbraith*

An elected official is one who gets 51 per cent of the vote cast by 40 per cent of the 60 per cent of voters who registered. *Dan Bennett*

89

PASTORAL CONCERNS

Any references to religion must obviously be handled with tact and discretion in any after-dinner speech, but that doesn't mean that light-hearted, well-meaning anecdotes and observations about the clergy or religious groups cannot be incorporated; it's a matter of using your judgement to ensure that no offence can be implied by what you are going to say.

Stories about anonymous clergy and nameless churches can be given added appeal if you locate them in a local church and cast the vicar in the lead. Again you will be giving spice and topical interest to your speech and provided the material is delivered with good humour, it's sure to be received with it.

Stories
An elderly and somewhat rotund bishop was experiencing difficulty in rising from a park bench, where he had paused during his stroll, when a little girl ran up and offered a helping hand.
'That's very kind of you, my dear,' he said, 'but are you sure you're strong enough?'
'Oh, yes,' she replied, 'I've often helped daddy out of his chair when he was far drunker than you.'

PASTORAL CONCERNS

The Bishop of Hereford was once dining at the table of a famous peer of the realm, who lived in the diocese.

'I don't know if you've noticed, bishop,' boasted his host, 'but I never go to Church.'

'Yes, I had noticed,' replied the bishop.

The peer, who was by now rather drunk, continued: 'And I'll tell you why I don't go — the place is full of hypocrites!'

'My dear sir,' said the bishop smiling. 'Please don't let that put you off. I'm sure we can make room for one more.'

In the middle of a fierce theological debate, Dean Swift lost his temper and turned to a stranger sitting next to him to ask: 'On which side are you, sir? Are you an atheist or a Deist?'

'Neither, sir,' came the reply, 'I'm a dentist.'

John Wilkes found himself in a similar debate with a Roman Catholic who challenged him with the question: 'Where was your religion before Luther?'

'Tell me,' said Wilkes, 'did you wash your face this morning?'

'I did indeed.'

'Then pray where was your face before it was washed?'

The Reverend Sydney Smith was told by a man whom he had just outwitted in a discussion, 'If I had a son who was an idiot, I would make him a parson.'

'Your father was clearly of a different opinion,' replied Sydney Smith.

Jokes

An Irishman nearing his end was visited by the village priest who knelt beside him murmuring a few prayers and then asked: 'Friend, do you know who died that you might have salvation?'

'Please, father,' whispered the dying man, 'is this any time for riddles?'

A Jewish mother was taking her small son for a walk along a beach when suddenly a terrific squall blew up, bringing with it crashing seas and furious winds. Before they were able to run to safety, the two of them were engulfed in a huge wave which carried the little boy off his feet and far out to sea. Overcome with grief, the mother sank to her knees and prayed that God might take her life instead, so that her son might live.

In answer to her prayer a second massive wave surged up the beach and left the boy lying alive and well beside his mother. Again she clasped her hands and said: 'Lord, this is truly a miracle. How can I ever repay you?'

Then, after another look at her son she added: 'Lord, before you go, there's just one thing — he did have a hat.'

An evangelist at a large public meeting was in full swing, urging hs listeners to beware the wrath of God on Judgement Day.

'I warn you,' he thundered. 'There will be a weeping and a wailing and a gnashing of teeth.'

At this point, a woman at the back of the hall stood up and shouted: 'Sir, I have no teeth.'

'Have no fear, madam' responded the evangelist. 'Teeth will, of course, be provided.'

Patrick's mother was a very devout Catholic, so it was with some trepidation that he summoned up the courage to confess his little secret.
'Hail Mary, Mother of Jesus!' shouted his mother. 'The shame of it, you've broken my heart. Fancy carrying on with a Protestant.'
'No, mother, I said prostitute.'
'Well thank the Lord for that.'

A philosopher and theologian were engaged in an earnest dispute, during which the theologian repeated a traditional argument that the philosopher was like a blind man in a dark room looking for a black cat that wasn't there.
'That's as may be,' said the philosopher, 'but the theologian would have found it.'

A young parishioner recently arrived in London asked his vicar in confidence whether he thought he could live an honest Christian life on twenty-five pounds a week.
'My boy,' the vicar said, 'that's all you'll be able to do.'

After knocking several times at a front door in his parish, a vicar left a card having written on it: 'Revelations 3:20'. ('Behold I stand at the door and knock; if any man hear my voice I will come in to him.')
The following Sunday, as the congregation was leaving after Matins, one of the younger ladies

handed the vicar an envelope. Inside he found a note that read: 'Genesis 3:10'. ('I heard thy voice in the garden and I was afraid, because I was naked; and hid myself.')

Quotations

It is now quite lawful for a Catholic woman to avoid pregnancy by a resort to mathematics, though she is still forbidden to resort to physics and chemistry. *H. L. Mencken*

Confirmation — one of the sacraments of the Church of England — tends to be a sort of spiritual sheep dip. *Lord Altrincham*

Imagine the Lord talking French! Aside from a few odd words in Hebrew, I took it for granted that God had never spoken anything but the most dignified English. *Clarence Day (From: 'Father is Firm')*

It is the test of a good religion whether you can joke about it. *G. K. Chesterton*

It often happens that I wake at night and begin to think about a serious problem and decide I must tell the Pope about it. Then I wake up completely and remember that I am the Pope. *Pope John XXIII*

The Church of England has never been famous for its friendliness to other people. The Church has always been a sort of refrigerator van on the back of the train. *Rt Rev. Edward Lowry, Dean of Salisbury*

QUESTION OF JUSTICE

The law may, as Mr Bumble suggests in *Oliver Twist,* 'be a ass ... a idiot', but we're all bound by it and most of us take care to stay on the right side of it. Even so the law and its officers, from policemen and traffic wardens to

A funny thing happened to me on the way here....

denizens of the Inner Temple and the High Court, are frequently the subject of jokes and stories — perhaps because this is about the only safe way for having a dig at an institution few of us understand and fewer still wish to cross.

For an after-dinner speaker legal stories are some of the easiest to adapt. Events involving policemen and speeding motorists can usually be translated to feature the speaker, or a friend, and the circumstances surrounding an amusing case in a magistrates, or higher, court can often be structured to give a personal feel to an anecdote.

Stories
Police in York found themselves with egg all over their faces a few years ago. After complaints from local people that there were drunken women lying in the main street, the police moved in and arrested six French dancers. When they got to the station, the girls explained that they were members of a prestigious dance troupe and were advertising their forthcoming show at the York festival.

A Yorkshire miner injured at work was advised by his Union to sue the Coal Board for damages. All the parties involved agreed before the hearing that the miner's claim was a strong one, but it was still necessary for the plaintiff to give his account of the circumstances surrounding the incident so that damages could be assessed.

Unfortunately the miner ignored the advice of his lawyer to be brief and to the point, and began to give an embellished version of events. After a few minutes the judge became a little irritated and addressing the man's lawyer, said:

'Presumably your client is conversant with "de minimis non curat lex"?'
The lawyer replied: 'My Lord, in Selby they speak of little else.'

After F. E. Smith had given a long explanation of a client's case, the judge turned to him and said sardonically:
'I must say Mr Smith that in spite of your long speech, I am really none the wiser.'
'Perhaps not, my Lord,' F. E. replied, 'but you are certainly much better informed.'

On another occasion, while defending a client on a charge of indecent exposure, F. E. Smith told the court:
'At the time, my client was as drunk as a judge.'
'Mr Smith,' interrupted the judge, 'I think you'll find the phrase is "as drunk as a Lord".'
'As your Lordship pleases,' replied F. E.

A man who was found guilty by the jury was asked by the judge: 'Before I sentence you, have you anything you wish to say?'
The man, who was obviously a fan of *Star Trek*, took a matchbox out of his pocket, held it up to his mouth and said:
'Right, beam me up, Scotty.'

The American advocate Max Steuer was another known for his courtroom wit. When he was called upon to apologise to the court one day by a boorish judge, he got his own back with this delightfully ambiguous comment: 'Your Honour is right and I am wrong, as your Honour normally is.'

Having spent over two hours besieging a gunman who was holed up in his own house, police in America fired tear gas through the windows only to discover that the man was standing beside them begging himself to come out and give himself up. Not surprisingly, he was sent to a psychiatric hospital for tests.

Mae West once said: 'It ain't no sin to crack a few laws now and then, just so long as you don't break any.' Probably the law which is most cracked in this country is the one governing income tax. It's certainly the most worried about. Earlier this century it was decided to give Joseph Conrad a knighthood, and the offer was sent to him in an official envelope bearing the words 'On His Majesty's Service'. The envelope lay unopened on the writer's desk for weeks. Eventually, a messenger was despatched from the Prime Minister's office to find out the reason for the delay. Apparently, Conrad had not opened the letter because he thought it was a demand from the revenue.

Jokes
Having made several appearances in a magistrate's court charged with vagrancy and disorderly conduct a down-and-out with a weakness for the bottle found his way to a higher court where the judge sought to rid him of his problem.

After hearing the man's pleas, the judge, a kind-

hearted man, decided to let him go. 'But I'm doing this on one condition,' he said. 'I want you to promise me that not another drink will pass your lips.'
'It won't, your honour, I promise — not one.'
'Not another, remember — not even the teeniest, weeniest sherry before lunch.'

A defendant charged with burglary in a delicatessen told the judge that he had only committed the offence because he was hungry.
'If you were that hungry,' said the judge, 'why didn't you just make yourself a sandwich instead of robbing the till.'
'I'm a proud man,' the defendant explained, 'I like to pay for what I eat.'

'How could you take this money from people who trusted you?' a judge asked a man charged with fraud.
'Because it doesn't work with people who don't trust you,' the defendant replied.

A persistent criminal was asked by a judge how many times he had already been convicted for the same offence. 'Five, my Lord,' he replied.
'Five. Then this time you will receive the maximum sentence.'
'But, your lordship — don't regular customers get discount?'

A judge giving his sentence to a notorious pickpocket asked him scathingly: 'Tell me what good you have done society.'

'I've kept four detectives working full-time,' the man in the dock replied.

A motorist apprehended by police after an accident was asked why he had been running away.
'I was trying to stop a fight,' he explained.
'But no one was fighting.'
'The other driver would have been if I'd given him a chance.'

Quotations

Courtroom: A place where Jesus Christ and Judas Ischariot would be equals, with the betting odds in favour of Judas. *H. L. Mencken*

The Lord Chief Justice of England recently said that the greater part of his judicial time was spent investigating collisions between propelled vehicles, each on its own side of the road, each sounding its horn and each stationary. *Philip Guedalla*

I think a judge should be looked on rather as a sphinx than as a person — you shouldn't be able to imagine a judge having a bath. *Judge H. C. Leon*

A witness can't give evidence of his age unless he can remember being born. *Judge Blagden*

I cannot help thinking that the English Bar is probably the oldest and tightest trade union in the world. *Sir Patrick Hastings*

Justice is too good for some people and not good enough for the rest. *Norman Douglas*

ROYAL PROGRESS

With the widespread interest in our royal family, entertaining stories about them rarely fail to delight an audience. Whether you tell a story of the Queen Mother displaying impeccable tact, or the Duke of Edinburgh

showing the benefits of a quick and lively mind, after-dinner material adapted from items dealing with royalty invariably goes down well with an audience.

The majesty of office itself lends a similar appeal to members of other royal families past and present. From those royal anecdotes that illustrate a particular weakness we all may be prone to when confronted with the great and famous, to ones that demonstrate how royalty have behaved in a perfectly natural way to save awkward situations or put others at their ease, royal material reveals a lot about human nature. Perhaps some of the items here will inspire you to start unearthing similar ones of your own.

Stories

During his long spell as Prince of Wales Edward VII impressed many people by his easy-going manner. One American at a reception attended by the prince who had been particularly struck by this com-mented to a fellow-guest: 'You know, he treated me as an equal.'

'Yes, His Royal Highness is always ready to forget his rank,' said the other man, 'as long as every one else remembers it.'

When the plans were being prepared for the celebrations marking Queen Victoria's Diamond Jubilee in 1897 it was discovered that the statue of Queen Anne outside St Paul's Cathedral not only blocked the way for the royal coach and its attendant horsemen, but it also obstructed the view of the huge crowd that was expected in the street outside. The organizers suggested that Queen Anne might be tactfully removed while the celebrations lasted but the Queen would not hear of it.

'What a ridiculous idea!' she said. 'Move Queen Anne? Most certainly not! Why it might some day be suggested that my statue should be moved, which I should much dislike.'

During the First World War, a young American officer was enjoying a quiet smoke in his hut when a British subaltern walked in.

'What are you doing?' snapped the American.

'I'm terribly sorry, old chap,' said the subaltern.

'And who are you anyway?' he asked.

'The Prince of Wales,' replied the subaltern calmly.

'If you're the Prince of Wales, I'm the King of England. Now get out,' shouted the officer.

A few days later, the two met again across a crowded Red Cross hut. On learning that the young subaltern really was the Prince of Wales, the American tried to slip away unnoticed, but was quickly spotted. The Prince, grinning widely, waved his hand in his direction and shouted:

'Hello there, dad!'

Towards the end of his life King George V came across one of his young grandsons engrossed in a book and asked what he was reading.

'It's a history book,' said the little boy.

'And who are you studying?' asked the king.

'Perkin Warbeck.'

'And who was he?'

'He's just someone who pretended he was the son of a king. But he wasn't really; he was the son of respectable parents.'

103

One day the King of Italy was walking in his garden with Mussolini who everyone knew was really running the country. As they discussed the affairs of state, the King accidentally dropped his handkerchief. Mussolini bent down to pick it up, knowing that protocol demanded as much, but the king prevented him from doing so with the words:
'Allow me. It's about the only thing I'm allowed to stick my nose in these days.'

Sir Malcolm Sargent, who had a particular fondness for patrons born with blue blood, once had a member of Scandinavian royalty present at one of his London concerts. In the interval he hurried round to the Royal Box to present himself and his leading soloist. 'Your Majesty,' he announced grandly, 'may I introduce Sergio Poliakoff? Sergio — the King of Norway.' The tall figure in the box shifted awkwardly and murmured: 'Sweden.'

The Queen Mother once told an interviewer that her favourite radio programme was *Mrs Dale's Diary*. When asked why, she replied:
'Because it's the only way of knowing what goes on in an average middle-class family.'

On one of her state visits to Australia, the Queen Mother was invited to attend a garden party. During the course of the reception, an increasingly large crowd began to gather round her peering with well-meaning curiosity. As the eager throng pushed and shoved, craning to get a better view, the Queen Mother was heard to say: 'Please don't touch the exhibits.'

Prince Philip once attended a dinner given by the Royal College of Surgeons. At the end of the meal, he was presented with a small silver cup, with the words: 'Your Highness, please accept this Bleeding Cup.'

The Prince looked at the cup, and replied:
'I can only say it is bloody kind of you.'

And if you want an amusing example of the Merry Monarch's wit that carries its historical veracity very lightly, here is an entertaining rhyme that captures the traditional fun of the Restoration court:

> 'Said Charles to his court, 'I enjoy a good port'
> But it must be a wine that's just right.'
> said a courtier game, 'If I tell you the name
> Of the best, will you make me a knight?'
> The King nodded his head, and the courtier said
> 'Cockburn's port is the port for a King;
> But remember to say it without the CK.'
> And the court cried 'Long live Harles the Ing!'

That may not have much to do with the real Charles the Second, but it will have a great deal to do with that stage of the dinner at which you are speaking and the port is circulating, and should reassure your audience that the mention of history need not be accompanied by a stifled yawn.

Jokes

Part of the charm of stories about royalty is that the personalities involved are usually fairly familiar to an audience. Jokes on the other hand are usually connected with unspecified people, which makes 'royal' jokes meaningless if they refer simply to 'a king' or 'a prince'. Any material like this is bound to sound hollow and will be counter-productive to any speech. Accordingly no 'royal' jokes have been included here.

Quotations

In a few years' time there will be only five kings in the world — the King of England and the four kings in a pack of cards. *King Farouk I of Egypt (two years later he was overthrown)*

There are always people around waiting for me to put my foot in it, just like my father. *Princess Anne*

A monarchy is a merchantman, which sails well, but will sometimes strike on a rock and go to the bottom; whilst a republic is a raft, which would never sink, but then your feet are always in the water. *Fisher Ames*

When Prince Andrew comes he always comes to the galley and waves at us and shouts 'Hallo slaves' — only as a joke of course. The Royal Family treat you like a person. *Bill Carbery, Steward of the Royal Train*

SUFFER THE LITTLE CHILDREN

'Out of the mouths of babes and sucklings, great truths do come.' I don't think that many parents would deny that there is more than a grain of truth in this old saying. For an after-dinner speaker addressing an audience, most of whom will either be parents or will know other people's families, it can be a passport to a world of innocent but delightfully profound observations on life and what adults make of it. Anecdotes, stories and other material centred on children can be turned to suit any number of purposes in a speech, providing an ironic commentary, revealing the contradictions of adult life, or simply giving voice to the hidden thoughts of others, to mention a few. Presented sympathetically and with as much personal detail and involvement as possible, this type of material can be used to great effect, while remaining pleasantly familiar to your listeners.

Stories
A mother, who was desperate that her four-year-old should be taken on at infant school even though the age limit there was five, was at pains to impress the headmistress with the child's ability to keep up with older children and assured her:

...then Rupert, my 7 year old, was so sickened by his 4 year old sister picking her nose and wiping it on the cat that he threw up into the custard... Well, as it was the same colour & grannie's eyes not being what they were.....

'I promise you she's as intelligent as any five-year-old.'

'Can you prove it by getting her to say something for us now?' asked the head.

'Certainly. Say a few words, dear,' prompted the mother

The girl looked at the headmistress, and then turned to her mother and said:

'What, something purely irrelevant?'

The young son of a famous actor was continually being asked by the adults visiting his nursery school the same inane question: 'And who's little boy are you?', after being pointed out to them by a member

of staff. Eventually his patience gave way, and he snapped back at one unwary enquirer:
'You know exactly who I am!'

A mother was suckling her new baby when her five-year-old son walked into the room and stared open-mouthed at the two of them. The mother could see that he was fascinated by what was going on, so she carefully explained the process by which women are able to provide milk for their babies. When she had finished, the boy looked at her and asked in a serious voice:
'That's all very well, but is it pasteurized?'

'Where do we come from Mummy?' a small boy asked. His mother was obviously embarrassed, so the child went on?
'Where did you come from, then?'
'Well, the stork brought me,' she answered hesitantly.
'Oh,' said the child, 'what about Daddy?'
'He was brought by the fairies,' replied the mother, more confidently this time.
'And me, who brought me?' the child continued.
'You weren't brought by anybody darling,' said the mother really warming to her task. 'You were found under a gooseberry bush.' Later that night, the child was finishing off an essay for his homework, and concluded:
'So, it appears that there have been no natural births in our family for years.'

Children can be at their most inspired when they make mistakes. This is especially true at school, as they are gradually introduced to new ideas and new words. The following examples are not only amusing, some can usefully be used as alternative quotations to illustrated points in your speech:

'Henry VIII spent most of his reign on the throne trying to produce a strong male heir.'
'An oxygen is a figure with eight sides.'
'The Sewage canal is in Egypt.'
'Electricity was invented by Voltaire, which is why it's measured in volts.'
'If you only have one husband, it's called monotony.'
'People who live in Paris are called Parisites.'
'Homer's most famous book is called The Oddity.'
'The Muslims have their own Bible called the Iran.'
'The future of "I give" is "You take".'
'Shakespeare wrote all sorts of plays — tragedies, comedies, and errors.'
'My mother doesn't call them napkins, she always says soviets.'
'I want to be an air hostage when I grow up.'
'In the future, we will be able to cure things with ultra-violent rays.'
'I think capital punishment does kids a lot of good.'

John D. Rockefeller's mother held a great respect for family discipline and whenever one of her children misbehaved, she was ready to offer a good hiding. One day John was on the receiving end of his mother's punitive zeal for an offence of which he was actually quite innocent. Before the spanking was over he managed to convince her that she was at fault, but she continued with the punishment saying: 'I may as well finish now I have begun. But it will be credited to your account the next time you are naughty.'

Jokes
'I hope you thanked Jamie's mother for the lovely party,' a mother asked her little boy after collecting him from a friend's house.
'No I didn't,' he replied. 'The girl in front of me thanked her and she said, "Don't mention it," so I didn't.'

A little boy was asked by a barber how he would like his hair cut.
'Just like Daddy's,' he answered, 'but please make sure you leave that little round hole on the top where his head comes through.'

'You must not stare at Uncle Michael,' a mother whispered to her small son whose eyes were fixed on the man sitting across the lunch table from him.
'But I don't understand, Mummy,' he said in a penetrating voice,
'I don't think he drinks like a fish.'

A little girl who saw a peacock for the first time rushed up to her mother and told her breathlessly:
'Quick, Mummy, come and look at this chicken in full bloom.'

A father was going through the family photograph album when he came across the picture of his wedding day. The little boy looked at the photograph of his mother in her wedding dress and,

111

pointing to it, asked: 'Was that the day Mummy came to work for us, Dad?'

'I hear God has brought you two lovely twin brothers,' a vicar visiting one happy family said to the little daughter.
'Yes', she said proudly, 'and what's more He knows where their school fees are coming from — I heard Daddy say so.'

'Mummy — do you remember that vase you were always worried I would smash?'
'Yes — why?'
'Your worries are over.'

A mother who went upstairs to kiss her little boy good night found his clothes scattered all over his bedroom floor. 'Who didn't hang up his clothes before he went to bed?' she asked trying to sound stern. 'Adam,' said her son, rolling over to go to sleep.

'And what are you going to do dear when you are as big as your Mummy?' an elderly friend asked a little girl whose family she was visiting.
'Diet,' said the child.

Quotations
Youth is a wonderful thing; what a crime to waste it on children. *George Bernard Shaw*

Children are given to us to discourage our better emotions. *Saki*

Reasoning with a child is fine, if you can reach the child's reason without destroying your own. *John Mason Brown*

Childhood shows the man as the morning shows the day. *Milton*

There was never a child so lovely but his mother was glad to get him to sleep. *R. W. Emerson*

A boy becomes an adult years before his parents think he does, and about two years after he thinks he does. *General Hershey*

THIS SPORTING LIFE

A great deal is revealed about people by looking at the way they use their free time and this is especially true of their attitudes to sports and games.

Obviously anyone speaking at a dinner connected with a particular sport or activity should try to include some reference to it, and time spent finding out about the personalities and past successes (or failures) of a club will be well rewarded.

With the principle of sport and fair play well rooted in our own heritage as well, you can modify material like that shown here to add a further dimension to a point you might be trying to make. Not that all our lives are conducted as cricket matches, but the way we face up to a 'sticky wicket' or settle into our 'innings' can be made that much more entertaining by broadening the range of subject matter and drawing some novel analogies.

Stories

Sir Leary Constantine used to tell the story of an occasion during a test match at the Oval when he was leaving the pavilion to start his innings and a phone call came through for him. As he passed the man who had taken the call, he heard him say: 'He's just going in to bat, will you hold on?'

Fred Trueman was playing in a match against the West Indies when one of the fielders dropped a catch in the slips, letting the ball race to the boundary for four runs. 'I'm sorry about that,' he said at the end of the over. 'Perhaps it would have been better if I had kept my legs together.'
'Yes,' commented Trueman, 'It's a pity your mother didn't.'

Two boys at Brighton College were reported by *The Cricketer* to have been suspended for gross disobedience. Their offence? They had very unwisely chosen to study for their imminent A-level exams, rather than play in the Headmaster's cricket team against the Old Boys.

A vicar whose passion for golf had made him as keen a disciple for the game as he was for the ministry tried for years to get a game off a partner without ever succeeding. His irritation built up steadily until one day he burst out saying: 'Why, oh why do I never win?'
'Don't get too upset, old chap,' replied his friend. 'You'll probably end up burying me one of these days.'
'I know,' said the vicar, 'but even then it will still be your hole.'

During a seven-a-side rugby tournament organized by the airline Cathay Pacific, the teams from Japan

115

and the USA found themselves lined up opposite each other. The Americans kicked off. The Japanese caught the ball, flashed it out to their wings and with some brilliant passing and running scored the first try. The Americans kicked off again. Again the Japanese gathered the ball, whisked it away and with more devastating play, ran in a second touchdown. After this had been repeated from the third place kick, the American coach was seen with his head in his hands murmuring: 'Pearl Harbour I can forgive. But not this!'

A few days before a very important football cup tie, it was reported in the local newspaper that one of the most ardent supporters of one club had died. By lunchtime the next day, four people had called at his house asking to buy his ticket.

An Englishman decided to watch the annual Glasgow Derby between Rangers and Celtic. It was a good match that year with both teams playing all out. Whenever Rangers scored, a huge cheer went up from their Protestant supporters; whenever Celtic retaliated, the Catholics were behind them. Both teams scored in quick succession just before the whistle at half-time and the Englishman, having no partisan feelings, cheered loudly for both. A Scotsman who had been keeping an eye on him since the kick-off, leaned over and asked: 'Good God, man. Haven't you any religion at all?'

Jokes
A golfer who kept losing his balls in the rough was

advised by his caddie that he might find it cheaper if he tried playing with old ones.

'That's all very well,' said the player, 'but I've never had a ball long enough to be old.'

A man who had been sitting beside a river without catching a single fish was asked by a little boy: 'How many fish have you got, mister?' The man told him. 'That's not so bad,' the boy said, 'there was a man here last time who'd been trying for two weeks and he hadn't caught any more than you've got in an hour.'

A soldier stationed in the desert, who had been an amateur swimming champion in his civilian days, was given a few hours leave one afternoon and was seen by his commanding officer striding purposefully across the sands in his swimming trunks.

'Where on earth do you think you are going?' shouted the officer.

'I just thought I'd go for a quick swim, sir,' replied the soldier.

'Are you out of your mind?' bawled the officer. 'The sea is 500 miles from here!'

'Yes. Lovely big beach, isn't it?' said the soldier.

A golfer who had just sliced his ball way off the fairway tried to blame his caddie for not having watched its flight.

'I'm sorry, sir,' said the caddie, 'but as it doesn't usually go anywhere, it sort of took me by surprise.'

Quotations

Ideally, the umpire should combine the integrity of a

117

Supreme Court Justice, the physical agility of an acrobat, the endurance of Job and the imperturbability of Buddha. *'Time' magazine*

Games are the last recourse of those who do not know how to be idle. *Robert Lynd*

There is one great similarity between music and cricket. There are slow movements in both. *Sir Neville Cardus*

If you watch a game it's fun. It you play it, it's recreation. If you work at it, it's golf. *Bob Hope*

I hate all sports as rabidly as a person who likes sports hates common sense. *H. L. Mencken*

As I understand it, sport is hard work for which you do not get paid. *Irvin S. Cobb*

U PON THE OPEN ROAD

The steering-wheel can sometimes bring out the worst in us as Mary Ellen Kelly implied when she observed: 'Natives who beat drums to drive off evil spirits are objects of scorn to smart Americans who blow horns to break up traffic jams.' Living in an age that would grind to a halt without the private car and lorry, we become victims, willing or unwilling, to fuel crises, mounting repair bills and motorway contra-flow systems. It's down this road that after-dinner speakers can run up against much of human nature in the raw, and be directed down another avenue that reveals further intriguing insights into what makes us tick.

Stories

A man who saw what seemed a perfectly good two-year-old car advertised in the local paper for £10 couldn't believe his eyes and rushed over to see it. He gave it a thorough examination and found everything in perfect working order. The woman selling it then showed him all the documents, and once again all was as it should be. Hastily giving her £10, he jumped into the driver's seat and started the engine.

'By the way,' he said before he drove it away, 'I must ask you why you're selling this car.'

'Simple,' replied the woman. 'My husband left me

this morning without a word and just gave instructions for me to sell it and send him the proceeds.'

One morning a young woman who had just passed her driving test got into her brand-new car to go to work. But the car wouldn't start. Not knowing what to do, she decided to ring for a mechanic. When he arrived, he lifted the bonnet, looked at the engine for a few seconds, and then gave one of the bolts on the battery a little twist. The engine started immediately.

'How much is that?' asked the woman.

'Five pounds and fifty pence please,' said the mechanic.

'I beg your pardon,' said the woman. 'That seems an awful lot of money for just twisting a bolt. How do you work that out?'

'It's like this,' replied the mechanic. 'Fifty pence for twisting the bolt, and five pounds for knowing which bolt to twist.'

Several years ago, police in Kent were phoned by a woman who claimed that she had seen a car driving past her house with two feet sticking out of the boot. Luckily, she had taken down the registration number, so the police were able to trace the car fairly quickly. The patrol car spotted it exactly as the woman had said, driving along with two feet sticking out of the boot. Once the officers had flagged it down, they approached the driver with caution. Suddenly, the two feet began to move, and a body emerged from the boot. It was the driver's mechanic

121

son listening for a rattling noise that only occurred when the car was in motion.

A vicar cycling round his parish before the war came to the help of a motorist whose car had overheated. He soon realized that the radiator had almost boiled dry.

'Since there's no water around,' he said unzipping his trousers, 'we'll have to make do with that with which the Good Lord has provided us.'

Looking carefully around to make sure no one else was about, he climbed on to the car's wing and peed into the radiator in the engine. This was not enough, so he turned to driver and said:

'I'm afraid that's all I've got. You'll have to have a go now.' At this the motorist removed her hat and dark glasses and said:

'I'd love to, but I'm afraid the Good Lord forgot to make the proper provision in my case.'

A couple from Surrey who had had their car stolen from outside their house found it returned three days later. When they looked inside it, they found two theatre tickets and a note which read: 'Sorry we had to take your car — it was an emergency.' The following week, they went up to London to use the theatre tickets. They had a wonderful time, but arrived home to find their house stripped from top to bottom.

Jokes

'I turned the way I signalled,' a learner driver complained indignantly after a minor collision at a junction.

122

'I know,' said the other driver, 'that's what threw me.'

Two men on a golfing tour of Scotland stopped to look at an ancient Celtic structure that was now little more than a pile of rubble. One of them suggested taking a snapshot and fetched his camera.

'Don't get the car in the picture,' said his friend in alarm as he was positioned in front of the ruin. 'If Alice sees that she'll think I've been trying to reverse again.'

A man driving a recently aquired rear-engine car ground to a halt by the side of a road and flagged down another motorist also driving the same model.

'I don't know a thing about cars,' he said, 'but it looks to me as if my engine has fallen out — there's nothing under the bonnet.'

'That's all right,' said the other man, 'I don't know much about cars either, but I know I've got a spare in the boot.'

'You were doing well over seventy miles an hour,' a policeman told a young motorist he had just pulled over.

'Really?' said the driver. 'Isn't that terrific and I only passed my test yesterday.'

Two driving instructors were discussing one of their less gifted pupils and one asked: 'Is he making any progress with you?'

'Well, the road is beginning to turn when he does,' said the other.

123

'Tell me what that other driver could have done to have avoided this accident,' a policeman asked a motorist who was clearly in the wrong.

'Well, he could have gone down another street,' he replied.

Quotations

After all, what is a pedestrian? He is a man who has two cars — one being driven by his wife, the other by one of his children. *Robert Bradbury*

No other form of transport in the rest of my life has ever come up to the bliss of my pram. *Osbert Lancaster*

A tourist is a fellow who drives thousands of miles so he can be photographed standing in front of his car. *Emile Ganest*

In the space age, man will be able to go around the world in two hours — one hour for flying and the other to get to the airport. *Neil McElroy*

The car has become an article of dress without which we feel uncertain, unclad and incomplete. *Marshall McLuhan*

Road: A strip of land along which one may pass from whence it is too tiresome to be to where it is futile to go. *Ambrose Bierce*

VENTURES ABROAD

Travel stories are a good example of the way that promising material can be made or marred in an after-dinner speech. A story set 'somewhere' on the continent, involving an unnamed person at an unspecified time, has nothing like the immediacy that might be gained by transferring the kernel of the story to your last family trip to Brittany a year ago, where an audience can easily relate to a first-hand experience of Common Market bureaucracy, the rekindling of the *entente cordiale,* or the resurgence of the Agincourt spirit. Names, places and events that have some identifiable meaning for an audience lend interest and inspiration — and with holiday and travel material the horizons are wide and inviting.

Stories
The artist James Whistler came across an Englishman having some difficuly in making himself understood in a Parisian restaurant. He offered to help with the order, only to be haughtily rebuffed by the man, who said he could manage perfectly well on his own. 'I fancied contrary just now,' said Whistler, 'when I heard you desire the waiter bring you a pair of stairs.'

Another Englishman on a visit to Paris, settled himself down for lunch in a cafe opposite Notre Dame, and ordered soup to start. When this came, the man noticed that there was a fly floating on the surface. Summoning the waiter, he explained the problem. Pointing at the offending insect, and saying
'Regardez — un mouche!'
The waiter began to shake his head.
'Non, monsieur,' he replied, 'C'est Une mouche. Feminine, n'est-ce-pas?'
'My word,' exclaimed the Englishman, 'you've got damn good eyesight.'

A similar episode with a fly happened to a woman travelling around Spain. She stopped to have something to eat in a cafe run by a poor Spanish family, ordered a traditional meal and followed it with a coffee. As she finished this, she noticed the fly at the bottom of her cup. Being a stickler for cleanliness, she shouted at the old woman serving her, 'What is the meaning of this?'
She came over to the table, and looked at the offending article. Raising up her hands in a gesture of apology, she replied:
'Señora, I'm sorry. I may be a Spanish peasant, but I'm not a fortune-teller.'

In Mexico, by a freak of nature, you sometimes find places where hot and cold springs exist literally side by side. An English tourist on a visit was being shown some of the sights by a Mexican guide when he noticed a group of women busy washing their clothes.

They washed them in the warm spring, and then rinsed them out in the cold one. The tourist was fascinated, and said to his guide: 'I suppose the women must thank Mother Nature for such useful coincidence?'

'Not really,' replied the guide. 'They spend their whole lives complaining that She hasn't provided any soap.'

A British businessman who arrived at a small hotel in India and asked for a room was immediately shown upstairs by the manager and offered the best one in the place. He accepted it willingly and asked the manager as he was leaving

'Don't you want me to register?'

'That is no problem, sir,' replied the Indian, 'I have already signed you in.'

'But you don't know my name,' protested the man.

'Yes I do sir,' answered the manager. 'I copied it off your suitcase.'

As he was paying his bill the next morning, the businessman was highly amused to find it made out to 'Mr Real Leather'.

Following his first holiday on the continent, a week in Dieppe, a Bradford man wrote to his local paper complaining that the French were a perverse race and there was little wonder that that Common Market was in the mess it was in. 'What can you do,' he asked, 'with a nation who arrange all their plumbing so that hot water always runs out of the tap marked "C"? I found this to be the case wherever I tried to wash my hands and in spite of numerous complaints no action was ever taken.'

Some of the most inspired examples of foreign English usage come from signs and notices, as these examples show:

Notice in Swiss hotel:
'In case of fire, please do all you can to alarm the hall porter.'

An advertisement for a French forwarding bureau:
'Put your luggage safely in our hands. We will send it in all directions.'

Notice in Spanish hotel bedroom:
'Please do not try to steal the towels. If you are not this person, stop reading.'

Notice in lobby of Belgian hotel:
'If you have any desires during the night, please do not hesitate to ring the receptionist.'

Notice in Japanese restaurant:
'Checked jackets may be worn, but *no* trousers.'

Jokes

A traveller touring India by train arrived at one town, disembarked and found he had to walk five miles from the station to the town centre. He finally got a lift in a tonga after struggling with his luggage for two miles. 'Why on earth did they build the station so far outside town?' he asked the tonga driver grumpily.
'So that it would be near the railway, sahib,' the man replied.

'Is this bus on time?' asked an irate passenger trying to travel from Rome to Florence by coach.
'No, mister, but it is on the right road,' the driver told him.

A tourist on holiday in Egypt decided to take a camel ride to look at some of the pyramids. Alone in the desert except for an Arab guide he became overwhelmed by the primitive romance of the barren wastes that lay all round. The pressures of his work and day-to-day concerns melted away, and for an afternoon he was transported into the world of Beau Geste and Lawrence of Arabia. At the end of the ride he tipped the guide generously and with a far-away look in his eye asked him: 'What is my camel's name?'
'Miss Piggy,' the guide replied.

'How much does it cost to take me to this hotel?' a tourist asked a taxi driver outside the main railway station in Athens.
'One hundred drachma, mister — your luggage, it go free.'
'Fine,' said the man loading his suitcases into the boot. 'Take these will you and I'll walk and meet you there.'

Quotations
In America there are two classes of travel — first class and with children. *Robert Benchly*

An Englishman's real ambition is to get a railway compartment to himself. *Ian Hay*

You'd think, with all these tourists about, they would build an elevator. *American lady overhead while climbing up to the Parthenon*

Airline travel is hours of boredom interrupted by moments of stark terror. *Al Boliska*

The heaviest baggage for a traveller is an empty purse. *English proverb.*

The great advantage of a hotel is that it's a refuge from home life. *George Bernard Shaw*

WAITER SERVICE

As an after-*dinner* speaker you will have to be careful about any references you make to food and catering. The last you want is for your hosts to get the impression that your remarks about poor food and shoddy service are being subtly directed at them. On the other hand, if you know from experience that the food and service are traditionally of a high standard, there is no reason why you shouldn't emphasize the point by giving some examples of how awful they can be in comparison, as long as you make your intentions absolutely clear.

The use of catering stories or jokes about wining and dining is a good example of a point emphasized throughout this book — the importance of freshness and familiarity in a speech. Anecdotes set in hotel dining-rooms or restaurants, jokes about incompetent waiters or inedible food, quotations about these or any related topics can be incorporated into a speech to provide a natural link between the dinner that has just ended and the speech or speeches that will follow. Used tactfully, with good humour and above all in circumstances where they are relevant, pieces like these provide valuable continuity in a speech.

Thatsa him, Godfather! He make-a-lotsa jokes about Italian waiters!

Stories

The playwright J. M. Barrie found himself once seated opposite George Bernard Shaw at a dinner-party. As the others were served with their meat course, Shaw, a vegetarian, was offered a selection of greens dressed with a mixture of salad oils. Seeing this concoction, Barrie could not resist leaning across and enquiring confidentially: 'Tell me, Shaw, are you about to eat that or have you already done so?'

Dining in a smart London restaurant one evening, during his time as a music critic, Shaw was enjoying his meal greatly until the orchestra struck up.

Seeing him at one of the tables, the conductor sent over a note asking if there was anything he would like the orchestra to play.

'Dominoes,' replied Shaw.

A young woman walked into a restaurant and ordered steak and chips.

'I'm sorry, we have no steak today,' replied the waiter.

'Then I'll have fish and chips!'

'The fish is off too I'm afraid.'

'What have you got?'

'Only sausages, madam.'

'Then I'll have sausages and chips, please.'

But the waiter had more bad news:

'By the way, there are no chips.'

'Well what do you have to go with the sausages?'

'Nothing madam; only a few kind words.'

The sausages arrived and the young woman tucked into them.

'What about those kind words?' she asked smiling, as the waiter was passing a minute or two later.

'I wouldn't eat the sausages,' he replied.

A group of corpulent businessmen at a sales convention were discussing a new advertising campaign late one night in one of their hotel rooms. Feeling peckish one of them ordered a plate of sandwiches. A waiter appeared almost immediately, but the sandwiches, daintily presented as triangles with the crusts cut off, did not last very long. They decided to ask for some more. 'Exactly how many would you like, sir?' asked the voice in room service.

'Well, let's see,' replied the man shrewdly, 'Judging by the size of the last lot and the size of this bill, I'd say about fifty pounds' worth.'

Confusion over cooking instructions can have unfortunate consequences in any kitchen. According to a newspaper report, the American Government are to change the way they tag migratory birds, after a little misunderstanding with an Arkansas farmer. The farmer in question shot one of the tagged birds as it flew over his land, and gave it to his wife to cook for supper. Unfortunately she mistook the tag round its leg for cooking instructions, and when supper was served neither of them could eat it. The words on the tag turned out to be an abbreviation of a Washington-based wild-life research survey — *Wash. Biol. Surv.*

Jokes

'Will you have red or white wine, sir,' asked a waiter in a restaurant.

'It doesn't matter to me at all,' said the diner, 'I'm colour-blind.'

'Would you mind changing this please?' a lady asked a waiter handing the cup from which she had just been drinking.

'What would you like, madam?' he asked, 'Tea of coffee?'

'If that's the tea, bring me coffee. If it's coffee bring me tea. Whichever it is I'd like it changed.'

'I want six hamburgers, please,' said a small boy at a take-away restaurant.

'What, all for you?' said the lady serving him.
'Don't be silly,' he said, 'I've got a friend waiting outside.'

'My butter is so strong that it could walk over and say hello to your coffee,' one diner confided to another at the next table.
'Well, if it did, it wouldn't get much response, the coffee is too weak to reply,' said the other.

'What's this leathery stuff?' asked a man eating at a newly opened fish restaurant.
'Fillet of sole, sir,' said the waiter grandly.
'Then could you take it away and bring me a nice tender bit from the upper part of the shoe?'

'Are you sure this milk is quite fresh?' a lady asked in a restaurant serving afternoon tea.
'Fresh? Madam, it was grass three hours ago,' came the reply.

Quotations

Dinner at the Huntercombe's possessed only 'two dramatic features — the wine was a farce and the food a tragedy.' *('The Acceptance World') Anthony Powell*

One meal a day is enough for a lion, and it ought to be for a man. *G. Fordyce*

Most people have a foolish habit of not minding or pretending not to mind what they eat. *Dr Johnson*

The English have a hundred religions, but only one sauce. *Voltaire*

135

At a dinner party one should eat wisely but not too well, and talk well but not too wisely. *W. Somerset Maugham*

The first of all considerations is that our meals should be fun as well as fuel. *Andre Simon*

X IS FOR EXERCISING THE MIND

Now we come to the third category of after-dinner entertainment mentioned in the Introduction — after-dinner games. These call for a very different type of evening than the more formal set pieces in which after-dinner speeches are given and enjoyed. Private dinner parties at home are a perfect setting for a variety of games that help extend the enjoyment centred on the meal itself late into the night around the fire.

In this first group come more cerebral games that can be played around the dining-table while the Cockburn's port is making its steady circumnavigation and while the last morsels of dinner are being savoured and the guests pause for a little digestive break before embarking on the more energetic games that follow.

Buzz-Fizz

Any number of players can play Buzz-Fizz, which is essentially a numbers game. Sit in a rough circle, and call out numbers in order one after the other — the first player calling 'One', the second 'Two', and so on round the table as quickly as possible.

You must, however, substitute the word 'Buzz' for the number 5 or any multiple of 5, and 'Fizz' for the number

7 or any multiple of 7. Thus 15 should be pronounced 'Buzz', 25 should be 'Buzz-Buzz', 28 should be 'Fizz', and 35 should be 'Buzz-Fizz'.

Any player who buzzes when he should be fizzing, or says a forbidden number drops out of the game. The last player left is the winner, though it is more likely to be two players left at the end buzzing and fizzing the night away.

Priest of the Parish

The players arrange themselves in a rough circle in the following order of precedence: the Priest of the Parish, followed by Matthew, Mark, Luke, and John. These are succeeded by the remaining players numbered from one onwards.

The game begins with the Priest reciting this strange incantation: 'The Priest of the Parish has lost his hat, and some say this, and some say that, but I say X has it.' (The blank is filled by one of the above names or numbers.) The Priest then counts quickly, but clearly, up to five, while whoever the Priest has named as the culprit then has five seconds to deny the charge. The denial must be recorded using these words: 'Not I, sir.' Variations such as 'Not me' or merely 'No' should not be allowed. If the denial is successful (and the Priest is the final arbiter on these things), the Priest then asks them: 'Who then, sir?' The alleged culprit then replies with a name or number of their own, and the process is repeated until someone makes a mistake.

A mistake occurs when:
1. A player speaks out of turn.
2. A player fails to make the denial within the time limit.
3. A player gets the words wrong.

If you make a mistake, you must move to the lowest position in the order of precedence, while everyone else moves up one. (It is quite legitimate to accuse the Priest of stealing his own hat.) When a mistake is made, the player occupying the Priest's seat re-starts the proceedings by reciting the sad news once again: 'The Priest of the Parish has lost his hat, etc.'

The aim of the game is to become the Priest, and remain the Priest.

Botticelli
One player thinks of the name of a famous person or fictitious character and reveals the first letter of his subject's name to the others. They then ask a series of *indirect questions* until he is unable to answer one. This allows the questioner to ask a *direct question,* which must be answered 'Yes' or 'No'. By this means the questioners gradually build up a portfolio of information about the character they are seeking until one of them discovers his or her identity.

Suppose the character chosen is Sir Christopher Wren. The player who opts for him tells the company that his character's second name begins with the letter 'W' — now they must discover the rest. They might ask indirect questions like: 'Are you an American president?' or 'Are you a famous English clergyman' to which the player asked the question has to reply, 'No, I am not George Washington,' or 'No, I am not Cardinal Wolsey.' If he cannot think of the name of an American president or an English clergyman whose name begins with 'W', the questioner might say, 'What about Woodrow Wilson?' or 'What about William Wyclif?' (there must always be a correct answer at the back of the questioner's mind). He is now in a position to ask a direct question: 'Are you

139

living?', 'Are you male?', 'Are you British?'. The correct answer must be given and the first clue is gained. The questions start again.

The more challenging the indirect questions, the easier it is to win *direct questions*. Once a player thinks he knows the identity of the mystery character he must pose an *indirect question* centred on that character, unless he has won the right to put a *direct question*. An *indirect question* on Sir Christopher Wren, for example, might ask: 'Did you design St Paul's Cathedral, the Royal Exchange and Greenwich Observatory ?' to which there is only one anwer: 'Yes, I am Sir Christopher Wren.'

Players who choose fairly predictable characters like Mrs Thatcher or Sir Winston Churchill have fairly short spells answering questions. Those who opt for slightly more challenging ones last rather longer.

Portmanteau

This is a memory game in which players have to remember an ever-increasing list of items chosen at random. The first player might begin by saying: 'I packed my portmanteau and in it I put *Dr Johnson's Dictionary.*' The second player takes up the list and says: 'I packed my portmanteau and in it I put *Dr Johnson's Dictionary* and a bottle of Cockburn's port.' Now the third player says: 'I packed my portmanteau and in it I put *Dr Johnson's Dictionary,* a bottle of Cockburn's port and a loufah.' And so the game proceeds with the list growing as each player adds one new item. When a player forgets one item or places one in the wrong order, he or she drops out. Play continues until only the winner is left.

X IS FOR EXERCISING THE MIND ———————

Lateral Thinking

Though Lateral Thinking problems are more like brain-teasers than normal games, they can be a very entertaining way of wiling the night away. One person presents the problem in the form of a story which then has to be 'solved' (or explained) by the others. They are allowed to ask questions though these questions can only be answered 'Yes' or 'No'. The accent is on thinking unusually, or laterally, since the problems are designed to resist conventional analysis.

1. A man lives on the twentieth floor of a block of flats. Each morning on the way to work, he takes the lift from the twentieth floor down to the ground floor. Each evening on the way back from work, he takes the lift to the tenth floor only. He then walks the rest of the way up to his flat on the twentieth floor. The man is always alone in the lift, and it is possible to get out of the lift on every floor. Can you explain his behaviour?

2. Anthony and Emma are lying dead on the floor. They are surrounded by broken glass and a few puddles of water. There is no blood and no suicide note. Can you explain how they died?

3. A man pushes a car up to a hotel. When he gets there, the realization dawns on him that he has lost all his money. Can you explain what is going on?

(Answers: 1. The man is a dwarf and cannot reach the lift button for the twentieth floor. 2. Anthony and Emma are goldfish whose bowl has been smashed. 3. The man is playing *Monopoly.* When his 'car' lands on a square with a hotel on it, the rent is too much for his resources.)

X IS FOR EXERCISING THE MIND————————————

Note: It is important that the stories are worded carefully so that they neither reveal nor conceal too much.

YOUR TURN NOW

From games played round the table with everyone still sitting we move into the sitting-room to play some slightly more active games that involve powers of physical expression as well as mental agility.

After a large and satisfying meal it is probably best to avoid anything too boisterous and the games given here can provide fun far into the night without leading to any unfortunate consequences.

Dumb Crambo

The company is divided into two teams. One team leaves the room and the other choose a word. When the outsiders return they are told a word that rhymes with the chosen one. They then guess the chosen word and mime an illustration of it. They may have three attempts and any player who speaks during that time forfeits the game for his team.

The Psychiatrist Game

One player leaves the room and is the 'psychiatrist', while the others decide on who is to act as the 'patient'. When the psychiatrist returns, he asks everyone including the patient the same three questions. These questions should

be designed to discover the identity of the patient, by building up an impression of his or her personality.

For example the psychiatrist might ask questions similar to these:

'What kind of animal does the patient remind you of?'

'What celebrity would this patient most like to be?'

'What would the patient do if he or she won a million pounds?'

'What single political measure would the patient most like to see taken?'

The patient must answer each question like all the other

144

players, though he must be careful to act as if he is not the patient. Once the psychiatrist has asked all three questions, he must guess the identity of the patient. It is then the patient's turn to go out of the room, and become the psychiatrist.

A couple of tips:
1. Be careful not to give the game away by looking at the patient as you answer the psychiatrist's questions.
2. Don't give away the sex of the patient. A man can wish to be Barbra Streisand as well as Clint Eastwood.

Proverbs
One player leaves the room, or goes out of hearing distance, while the remainder decide on a proverb. When the player returns, his task is to discover the proverb chosen by the others. He does this by asking each of them a question in turn. This question can be about anything he likes. The first answer must contain somewhere in it the first word of the proverb, the second answer the second word, and so on. If you get to the end of the proverb and the questions are still coming, simply go back to the first word of the proverb again.

If you decided on 'Don't rock the boat' as your proverb, the dialogue might go like this:

'What's your name?'
'If you *don't* know my name by now, there's something wrong.'
'Do you like music?'
'Yes, anything from soul to jazz, and *rock* to classical.'
'Are you married?'
'No, but that could be *the* proposal I've been looking for.'
'Where are you going on holiday this year?'

145

'We haven't decided yet. My wife wants to take a *boat* round the Greek Islands, and I want to go to New York.'
'What time is it?'
'I *don't* know, I haven't got my watch on.'

The questioner must guess the proverb within a specified time limit, say three minutes. To avoid making the answers too obvious, you must choose a proverb without too may awkward words. The words 'cook' and 'broth' in the proverb 'Too many cooks spoil the broth', for example, might be difficult to conceal, though this problem can be partially overcome by including some red herrings from other proverbs to put the questioner off, like 'bird', 'cloud' and 'silk'.

Charades
The players are divided into teams, the first team retiring to another room to choose a word they are going to dramatize and planning the performance they are going to give. The team captain then returns and tells the others how many syllables there are in his team's chosen word. The team then returns and various members act, with or without dialogue, little scenes depicting a clue to the sound of the syllables they are describing. Each syllable is acted individually and lastly the whole word is acted. The rest of the players watch and try to guess each syllable as it is being acted.

An exciting variation of this traditional format is for a team to decide on the title of a book, a play, a poem, a film, a piece of music, or a radio or television programme — with more than one word if they like. They then work out how this might be acted either with words, or much more amusingly as a dumb-show. Suppose the title chosen was *Julius Caesar*. The first part might be represented by

146

players examining their fingers and polishing imaginary rings (jewel). The second part might have players reaching up as far as they can (high). For the third part they might mime riding (horse). That takes care of *Julius*. The first part of *Caesar* might show the players laying hands on each other or one player in particular and holding on tightly (seize). And the final part could be conveyed by the action of rowing (oar).

When this plan has been decided, the players go back to the others and act out each scene. If their opponents guess the title before the charade is completed, they are the winners — not that this matters since it is their turn to perform the next one in any case.

In small groups or those where the players prefer to play as individuals, you can play 'Solo Charades'. This follows exactly the same rules, but the players take part individually.

The Railway Carriage Game

You need four or more players for this game. Two are selected and each is given a secret phrase. One might be: 'To be or not to be', the other 'Stop me and buy one'. Both players then climb into an imaginary railway carriage and chat for five minutes. During that time each must try to slip his or her phrase into the conversation as discreetly as possible. At the end of the five minutes each must guess the other's phrase, while the other players are rolling about with laughter!

ZIZZING

'And so to bed,' as Samuel Pepys recorded in his diary. The party over, the speech delivered (triumphantly we trust) sleep beckons the weary host or after-dinner speaker as memories of the evening merge and fade into oblivion and he nods off with the satisfaction of having given pleasure to others, the most enduring reward of all after-dinner entertainment — unless, of course, his name is Macbeth. As Shakespeare was at pains to point out, his Scottish host was a walking disaster when it came to fostering bonhomie, and he paid a terrible price, turning insomniac, for ever deprived of sleep the 'chief nourisher in life's feast'. How different his fate might have been if his 'vaulting ambition' had been directed to the goals set out in this book.

Whether in creating an atmosphere of relaxed conviviality where conversation can sparkle like the crystal, or in delivering an after-dinner speech that perfectly captures the mood and spirit of the evening, or even in selecting the right games that allow everyone present to shine, it is a sensitivity and awareness of the needs and interests of others that establishes the master (or mistress) of after-dinner entertainment.

To return to Samuel Pepys, writing this time before he

turned in on 9 November 1665: 'Strange to see how a good dinner and feasting reconciles everyone.'

If he had read this book, I like to think that he wouldn't have found it strange at all.